THE ESSENCE OF
Cognitive Psychology

THE ESSENCE OF PSYCHOLOGY SERIES

THE ESSENCE OF
Cognitive Psychology

Helen Gavin

An imprint of **Pearson Education**

Harlow, England · London · New York · Reading, Massachusetts · San Francisco
Toronto · Don Mills, Ontario · Sydney · Tokyo · Singapore · Hong Kong · Seoul
Taipei · Cape Town · Madrid · Mexico City · Amsterdam · Munich · Paris · Milan

Pearson Education Limited
Edinburgh Gate
Harlow
Essex CM20 2JE

and Associated Companies throughout the world

Visit us on the World Wide Web at:
http://www.pearsoneduc.com

First published 1998 by
Prentice Hall Europe

Typeset in 10.25/12 pt Plantin Light
by Photoprint, Torquay

Printed and bound in Great Britain by
Bookcraft (Bath) Ltd., Midsomer Norton, Somerset

Library of Congress Cataloging-in-Publication Data

Gavin, Helen
    The essence of cognitive psychology / Helen Gavin.
        p.   cm.
    Includes bibliographical references and index.
    ISBN 0–13–796459–5 (alk. paper)
    1. Cognitive psychology.   I. Title.
BF201.G38   1998
153—dc21   97–44936
                                                                 CIP

British Library Cataloguing in Publication Data

A catalogue record for this book is available from the British
Library

ISBN 0–13–796459–5

---

10 9 8 7 6 5 4 3 2
06 05 04 03 02

This book is dedicated to Martin, for providing the space in which to write it, and having patience whilst it was written.

Contents

Preface

This book was written to provide its readers with basic information about Cognitive Psychology. It is an introductory text aimed at foundation level psychology undergraduates, or possibly 'A' level students, and anyone who has an interest in the working of the mind.

Taking an imaginary journey through a system of cognitive functions, the reader follows information as it enters, interacts with and leaves the cognitive structures. In this way an often difficult and obscure subject will be made clear, and abstract concepts made more concrete.

The book takes a mainly historical perspective, setting the scene and discussing the development of the subject. However, several modern thoughts and pieces of research are discussed in the context of the established findings.

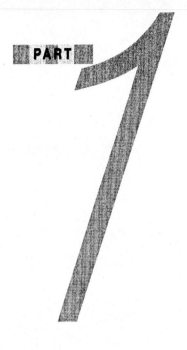

Background

This part covers the background to the study of the human mind, and identifies its scope and intent. Chapter 1 sets the scene and explains what this book is about, and Chapter 2 looks at the development of Cognitive Psychology, and its contemporary viewpoints.

Introduction

Key terms

cognitive system the structure that deals with information
ecological validity the ability to generalise results from a study across a variety of settings
empiricism the acquisition of knowledge through experience
experimentation a research approach in which attempts are made to identify causal relationships among variables under controlled conditions
information processing the mental activity of operating on information; an approach to studying cognition
introspection the consideration of the contents of one's mind, and the reports of that consideration
rationalism the acquisition of knowledge through reasoning

Key names

Descartes • Hume • James • Kant • Popper • Wundt

What is Cognitive Psychology?

Psychology deals with many aspects of human activity, from the most social of interactions, to the most private of thoughts. Cognitive Psychology is that area dealing with mental activities in the processing of world and individual information. Our concern here is how the human system senses information and acquires it, and how the information is transferred and transformed inside the system. For the purposes of explanation we need to picture an imaginary structure, which gets information from the environment, and deals with it in particular ways, until it is acted upon or stored (or lost), then expressed. This structure is to be called the cognitive system.

This book will introduce you to Cognitive Psychology by taking an imaginary trip through the cognitive system, following information as it is received, how it is then dealt with and processed, stored and used. It will

3

examine research that has attempted to investigate this path and process. In this way we will endeavour to answer the major questions of Cognitive Psychology:

▶ How do we acquire information?
▶ How do we deal with information?
▶ How do we remember?
▶ Why do we forget?
▶ How do we think?
▶ How do we solve problems?
▶ How do we express our thoughts and deliberations?

History of Cognitive Psychology

Great thinkers throughout history have pondered on the very concept of thought. Much of Greek philosophy is concerned with human knowledge, its form, and its origin. Plato's dialogues include empirical observations of the use of knowledge, and conclusions about its source. Later philosophers who have also had great effect on the study of knowledge and thought include Descartes, Hume and Kant.

Descartes' contribution to philosophy was wide-ranging, but his influence on the study of thought was the introduction of the idea of mental structure. As a rationalist, he believed that knowledge was acquired through reasoning. Through the application of such an approach he inspired the method known as introspection. This method involves the examination of one's own mind and its contents, and was a major technique in the early development of psychology.

Hume, on the other hand, was an empiricist. Empiricism states that knowledge is acquired through experience. Hume's contribution to the development of Cognitive Psychology was his pursuit of the laws by which ideas are associated, and the classification of the mind's operations.

Kant identified both mind and experience as sources of knowledge, proposing an approach based on both rationalism and empiricism. Stating that the mind provides structure, and experiences provide facts to fill the structure, he distinguished three kinds of mental structure we will encounter repeatedly in the study of cognition: dimensions, categories and schemata.

These three philosophers are by no means the only people to have had an impact on modern Cognitive Psychology, but these views will be seen to be influential.

Psychology is based upon as much conceptual analysis and speculation as philosophy. Where it differs is in the use of experimentation. Early psychologists were trained in the 'natural' sciences, but became fascinated by the structures of the mind. Wundt was originally a physiologist, who founded the first laboratory, in Leipzig, to apply observation and empirical methods to the study of behaviour in a systematic way. Similarly James was originally qualified in medicine. He was working at the same time as Wundt, but in the USA, and wrote perhaps the first modern psychology textbook. He based the book on his work in the systematic study of psychological phenomena, but he attempted to take this investigation out of the laboratory. His research had real application, principally in the field of education.

Many such instances of the influence of other disciplines and sciences can be found in the history of psychology, particularly the study of cognition. These influences and developments are discussed in detail in Chapter 2.

Criticisms of the Cognitive Psychological Approach

The types of issues studied by cognitivists do, of course, demonstrate one of the difficulties with Cognitive Psychology, in that it deals with internal events or processes. It is the study of behaviour in terms of events occurring within a person. We do not view behaviour as simply a response to a stimulus, because of this notion of internal events. These are referred to as mediators, and include such things as perception, problem solving, memory, and internal representation of language. This concept requires some thought and even imagination, combined with rigorous research techniques, like controlled experimentation. There are also other problems with the cognitive approach.

Unlike other areas, Cognitive Psychology appears to lack integration. There is no particular framework, and no one particular theory that we can point to, and say 'that is cognition, and that is the major theorist'. There is no one distinct theme, such as the stage theories of Developmental Psychology. Cognitive Psychology therefore is not so much a theory or set of theories, as an approach to psychology that stresses mental processes and how they might affect our behaviour and interactions with the world. In turn, though, this means that not only can we consider a Cognitive Psychological explanation of perception and thinking, etc., but we can use the approach to understand emotion, and social functioning too. So a problem that at first might make the area appear difficult to study, actually demonstrates its flexibility.

Another major criticism is the idea of a person as a machine, or a system, the metaphor that many cognitivists use. This seems offensive to many, even to psychologists, who argue that the fundamental differences between human and machine are not being addressed. The thing to remember is that this is a metaphor, a useful way of describing items in ways we understand. There is no suggestion that a human is anything other than an amazing organic creation. In studying cognition we view processes as operating systematically rather than randomly. This leads many working in the field to use a computer metaphor when describing human processing, referring to people as information processors. We appear as entities that absorb information, code, interpret, store and retrieve it. This works both ways. Take an introductory course in computing as a psychology student, and you may find yourself thinking of computer components in terms of their organic 'equivalents'. However, we can recognise a metaphor for what it is, a useful way of imagining a complicated structure, and not take it too far. This is because we are human, and can use our cognitive system to reflect upon itself, even if it is not directly observable.

The final major criticism is with the experimental approach itself. Many researchers argue that it is 'artificial' and not representative of events in the real world. Contemporary cognitive psychologists endeavour to overcome this criticism by increasing the *ecological validity* of their work. This is an attempt to describe the use of information in everyday, significant situations. It also hopefully means that the theories and findings of cognitivists are explained in everyday, meaningful language.

Strengths of the Cognitive Psychological Approach

Cognitive Psychology as an approach has contributed much to our understanding of the mind. There are several ways in which it has done this. The first is in the development of theoretical models that attempt to explain in detailed ways what has resulted from the examination of behaviour and function. This is in contrast to the broader theories of other areas of psychology. What the cognitive theories have in common is the possibility of *falsifiability* (see the section on studying cognition below) and hence the possibility of progression as ideas are adapted, modified, or even abandoned. The theories are also durable, they stand the test of time and can advance. Other areas have durable theories too, but in some cases these theories survive because there is a lack of viable alternatives, or because they simply cannot be subjected to rigorous examination. A theory that is never wrong is not necessarily always right. Some theories in the cognitive area do fall foul of this, but we will examine them in the light of our precepts. So Cognitive Psychology and most of its theories are robust and durable.

Cognitive Psychology has made some tangible contributions too, not just the insubstantial, ephemeral contribution of advancing the cause of science. Due to the pursuit of knowledge in this area, alongside the study of areas such as neuropsychology, we have very concrete knowledge about how the brain works, and how damage (physical or psychological) affects it. We have major insights into problems such as amnesia and learning difficulties. We must remember that no discipline or approach is isolated from others around it. Such is true of Cognitive Psychology. Drawing in knowledge from other areas is always possible when the method applied is robust. Contributing to other fields is feasible when the results of studies hold up to scrutiny. It might borrow, but it also lends.

Studying Cognition

So, how can we study the ways in which people access and use information when those processes are not observable? For example, we cannot see memory working, we can only observe the effect of its success or failure. Experimentation, with its elements of control and inference, is one of the most useful approaches in Cognitive Psychology. A great deal of the work in cognition has involved the construction of theoretical models tested by experiments. It would be useful therefore to briefly revise what experimentation actually is.

The Experimental Approach

Experimentation has as its basis the elements of observation, inference, control and comparison. It attempts to build a relationship between what we see happening, what we think is happening, and how we might test the resulting theory. So, for example, we might observe that it is possible to remember a telephone number in the period between hearing it and reaching a telephone, so long as nobody asks the time on the way. This leads us to ask 'does distraction affect the retention of long numbers?'. We can test this by comparing two situations that are as identical as we can make them. In one the participants hear numbers, experience a waiting period, then are asked to recall. In the other they are distracted by another task. Any difference between performance in the two situations (or *conditions*) leads us to infer that the distraction has had an effect. This simple *design* is the basis of experimentation, and it is a useful tool in studying cognition, in that it allows us to examine human performance. Our basic experiment here would test volunteers' ability to recall simple sequences of numbers or words, after they had been subjected to a distraction task, or not. A significant difference in the ability to recall in the two conditions would lead us to accept the hypothesis '*distraction has an effect on recall*'. If we found no significant difference, then we would reject our hypothesis. In this way we can test hypotheses, and relate them back to theoretical models. Such an approach also allows us to open our theory up to the possibility of *falsifiability*. Popper (1959) stated that if a theory is to be a good theory, then we have to be able to see how we can prove it false. Not that we actually have to prove it false, just that it should be possible to do so. The classic example of this is the white swan hypothesis. If we think that all swans are white, we cannot prove that this is true. Every instance of a white swan verifies the idea, and adds to our conviction, but without seeing every swan in existence now, in the past and in the future we cannot completely prove this true. But we can prove it false, by seeing one black swan. On the other hand, consider the belief that Elvis Presley is alive and well. Can this ever be proved true? Presumably by the reappearance of the man himself, although he may be an impostor. Can it be proved false? Reports of his death may have been fabricated, the body lying in Gracelands cemetery may not be his, and so on. So in order to examine and verify a theory, we need to use a method by which we can see a way out of the vicious circle of collecting evidence and then refuting it. Classical experimentation allows this as it sets up a direct comparison between the conditions. However, this method has been criticised for its lack of *ecological validity*. This is the ability of theories to describe what happens in everyday situations. Whilst this does not mean that we necessarily reject the use of laboratory-based data collection, we do have to be able to relate what we find to the outside world, i.e. real life. The benefit here is that cognitive psychologists now strive to explain theories and the testing of them in understandable ways, relating the finding to commonly experienced circumstances. It also means that we are less likely to see experiments such as making rats run around mazes being related to human behaviour. Let the rats do whatever rats do, and leave them alone.

A point to note here too, is that a 'natural' setting does not necessarily mean that a study has ecological validity. That naturalistic study might not generalise to other settings. Also consistent laboratory-based findings must be explained, somehow. Natural is not necessarily good, and laboratory is not necessarily bad, but meaning is everything.

The Hypothetical Model Approach

An alternative methodological approach is that proposed by Hebb (1949). His work was in the nervous system. He showed that it was not necessary to have complete knowledge about the central nervous system, as even sophisticated neurosurgical techniques cannot allow us to discover everything. He proposed that until complete knowledge was available, we can construct hypothetical models of the way in which systems work. Testing these models allows them to be supported, adapted or replaced, in much the same way as hypothesis testing in the laboratory also allows knowledge to progress. This approach is very useful in Cognitive Psychology, and allied disciplines/fields of study such as Artificial Intelligence. We will examine examples of models and the research carried out upon them later in the book.

The Scope of Cognitive Psychology

Given the strengths and weaknesses of this area of psychology, what we need to know now is the nature of the subject that we are studying. If we allow that there are problems, we also know that there are benefits, but what is it that we gain? One major viewpoint in Cognitive Psychology is termed the information processing approach, due to the machine metaphor described above. This book follows this approach, but will also examine allied viewpoints (see

Chapter 2). The information processing view looks at the human cognitive system as something that has input, storage, throughput and output. This is the way in which we will examine the cognitive system, through the areas outlined below.

Cognitive Psychology covers several principal areas: perception, attention, memory, knowledge, language, and cognition other than human. These can be described as information gathering and input, information storage and organisation, and information use. Each of these stages of information in the system makes one major part of this book.

Part 2

Perception is concerned with the way in which information reaches the cognitive system. In order to understand this, we need to understand the perceptual system, and how we interpret sensory signals. Stimuli can be of several different types or modalities, so Chapter 3 will describe how sensations are perceived. We will then examine pattern recognition. Items coming in to the system are unlikely to be solitary events, so they are perceived as parts of an overall pattern. We need to know how this can happen, and how the perceptual system works to allow this.

There are several theoretical models of how information reaches the cognitive system and is selected for further processing. These models of attention will be examined in Chapter 4 by looking at the proposed ways in which information reaches the cognitive system. Chapter 5 examines how our awareness of information affects how we deal with it.

Part 3

Once information has reached the cognitive system it must be processed into other forms. There are four chapters on memory, outlining structure, processing and storage, remembering and forgetting. Chapter 6 looks at the postulated structures that memory takes, and compares theoretical models. Chapter 7 follows the processing or encoding of information to stored forms, and the retention and retrieval of information. Chapter 8 is concerned with memory failure. For stored information to be useful, it must be acted upon and transformed. Chapter 9 looks at the ways in which information is transformed into knowledge and how this is organised and represented.

Part 4

The next point in the chain is how knowledge structures might be navigated in order to gain access to them. Concepts and mental models are several ways in which knowledge is organised, and we examine them in relation to the way we use our knowledge. We need to look at logic and decision making, and the output of that – problem solving and reasoning – in Chapter 10. The measurable activity of knowledge use we call intelligence or even creativity, and Chapter 11 discusses these areas. We also need to learn our knowledge and the allied performance of its use, cognitive skill. Skill and expertise are explored in Chapter 12.

In humans, and arguably in other species, thoughts, the product of acting upon stored knowledge, are expressed in language. The final chapters in this part cover the major theories in the acquisition of language and its development, together with the perception and analysis of language (comprehension).

Part 5

To avoid becoming too concentrated on the human, we should also look outside. The final chapters will look at animal cognition, seeking to think about what we can learn from examining cognition other than our own (Chapter 16), and machine cognition: what can we build with what we know (Chapter 17)?

In this way, we can follow a journey through the human cognitive system, from outside stimuli, through acquisition of information, and how we act upon it, store it (or lose it), navigate what we have stored, use it, and express it. Hopefully you will find that this is done in a way that explains the cognitive approach in terms that are not jargon based, and not obscure, and that the information is then summarised in an unambiguous and clear way.

How to Use this Book

Each chapter is relatively short, and takes one specific topic at a time. In this way each area can stand on its own, and be examined in isolation, but links to other areas are also spelt out. In order to facilitate learning, for after all you are likely to be reading this in preparation for assessment of some kind, there are mnemonics and helpful summaries included as you go along.

> mnemonic a technique assisting or designed to assist memory

In addition to these hints in the text, at the beginning of each chapter is a list of the researchers whose work is explored in the chapter, together with a glossary. And if that still does not help you, there are self-test questions at the end of each chapter, with answers or suggested answers at the end of the book.

Approaches to Cognitive Psychology

Key terms

associationism a theory of cognitive functioning in which learning and thinking consists of a sequence of experiences linked via various principles

behaviourism a theory of functioning in which learning, thought and behaviour are the result of stimulus–response relations

connectionism a theory of cognition allied to associationism, but which emphasises the strength and type of connection between elements

Gestalt theory and principles German – 'configuration'– a theory which states that experience is coherent and unified

human performance/human factors a research approach based on studying the factors which affect performance

information processing the mental activity of operating on information; an approach to studying cognition

mental chronometry measurement of the time taken to perform mental processes

psychophysics measurement of, and the development of general laws to describe, relationships between psychological experience and changes in continuums of stimuli

Key names

Broadbent • Chomsky • Fechner • James • McClelland and Rumelhart • Neisser • Skinner • Thorndike • Turing • Watson

There are several different ways to look at cognition. This chapter will examine the various approaches to studying cognition in depth – psychophysics, associationism, Gestalt, information processing and connectionism.

Psychophysics

As we know, modern psychology is the child of philosophy and physical sciences. Just as Wundt and James (see Chapter 1) were originally physiologists who became interested in mental processes, so do we find that physicists were also interested in the relation between body and mind. Bringing their laboratory methods to this new science allowed the formal investigation of psychological phenomena. Fechner, a physicist, examined the way changes in stimuli were related to psychological experience. He looked at perceptual thresholds: for example, the absolute threshold is the point at which a participant can detect a tone; the difference threshold is the point at which a participant can detect the difference in two stimuli. It was found that the latter is relative – if the comparison between two items is made with the original stimulus being small. For example, if you put a penny into someone's palm, then add another, the participant will notice the difference, but if you start with 50 pennies, and add one, the difference is unlikely to be noticed. Such experiments led to the development of laws that can be represented algebraically. Whilst psychophysics is not really concerned with internal mental events, the research methods are very useful, and the laws developed are of great value.

Associationism

A very ancient theory, the associationist tradition is based on the premise that we are born with very little knowledge, our minds are blank slates upon which the world can write. The idea is that our mental structure becomes a network of *associations* between items of information as we experience our environment. So, when a child plays with a kitten, she notices that it is soft. These two experiences become linked together, or associated. The next time she feels something soft, she thinks of the kitten, and perhaps even says so. As we become older, and experience more things, the network becomes more complex, and our use of it more sophisticated.

Scientific study of associationism began most notably with Thorndike (1898). He used cats in experiments designed to show how they manage tasks by building associations. It is not recorded whether or not he noticed the cats were soft. He placed cats in boxes in which the door can only be opened by moving a stick hanging from the ceiling. The cat will eventually do this, but rather than developing understanding of the relation between stick and escape, the cats appear to accomplish the task by trial and error. Accidentally brushing against the stick gives escape, so the cats form an association between the two, but do not operate at any higher level than this simple link.

The introduction of behaviourism in the early 20th century led to further notions about the organisation of the mind. Watson was an extremely influential person in this field, and in his 1930 book, *Behaviourism*, he actually stated that the blank mind of a child could be shaped in whatever way an adult wished, given a specialised and enclosed environment. Skinner was also a major figure in this area, who took behaviourism to perhaps its most extreme form. He believed that cognition is purely a set of stimulus–response (S–R) relationships, rather than some nebulous, obscure mental activity. Skinner said that thinking consisted of a series of small scale behaviours, happening, admittedly, where we cannot see them, but just the same as external behaviours, controlled by the environment and the stimuli received from it.

Due to the influence of psychologists like Watson and Skinner, much of the scientific study of psychology in the first half of the 20th century concentrated on analysing associations, particularly between directly observable stimulus–response relations. Associationism attempts to explain behaviour by links between what is experienced. For example, consider copy-typing. Each letter on your hand-written version of that essay you have to type up for submission is associated with a key on the keyboard. So the hand-written stimulus letter is associated with a particular key. As you become more adapt at typing, sets of letters become quicker to type. Words, and even sentences, are typed more quickly. An associationist would explain that each response (a key) becomes the stimulus for the next and so on – an associative chain. This is a very attractive explanation, until we consider errors in the process. Sometimes responses happen out of sequence in the chain. In our typing example, it often happens that even experts make anticipatory errors, so that instead of typing 'cognitive psychology' we see 'pcognitive psychology' on the page. It appears the p of psychology has been primed or activated before it is needed. A well-known phenomenon of this sort is Spoonerisms.

Spoonerism a verbal error named after Dr Spooner, a 19th century British academic with a reputation for comical blunders. On one occasion, instead of raising his glass to the Dear old Queen, he toasted the 'Queer old Dean' – allegedly

More seriously, there are other major criticisms of associationism. Skinner had stated that language is processed in this simple S–R fashion. Chomsky (1959, see the chapters on language) criticised this assertion, pointing out that language is often used creatively. We very often use sentences that are unique, and have never been heard before in precisely that form. Associationism would mean that every word in a sentence must be associated with all of its companions, surely an impossible task even for a huge and complex network. Chomsky argued that language must be under the control of some central process, rather than a peripheral process involving only the S–R linkages. This and other criticisms of associationism mean that research in psychology started to concentrate on cognitive processes.

Gestalt

Gestalt is a German word meaning configuration, and Gestalt psychologists believe that experience is unified and coherent, and that it cannot be understood by simply breaking it down into its constituent parts. A famous phrase associated with Gestalt theory is that 'the whole is greater than the sum of its parts'. Each item in the world has meaning beyond the parts of which it is made. Thus a melody is not simply a sequence of musical notes, and a triangle is not merely three joined lines. An example of this idea can be seen in *perceptual restructuring*.

perceptual restructuring the experience of seeing two pictures in one. In certain drawings there is an effect of perception shifting from seeing one thing to seeing another

According to Gestalt theory, we perceive items as a coherent whole. The way in which this is examined is by using a phenomenological approach. This means that participants in studies were asked to report on perceptual phenomena they experienced, and psychologists developed what are known as Gestalt principles. These principles are proximity, similarity, continuation and closure. These are demonstrated by the items in Figure 2.1. A shows a set of shapes in an array. B is the same number of shapes, but we see them as columns. Objects in close proximity are perceived as being grouped. C shows how similar characteristics lead us to perceive items as grouped; here it is the different colours that influence our perception. In D we see the lines as uninterrupted, showing the perception of continuation. Finally E is perceived as being complete even though we know a line is broken. We fill in the gap, demonstrating closure.

Gestalt theory also contents that our current experience is not influenced by past learning. Consider Figure 2.2. There are black circles with shapes cut from them. The cut-outs appear to be circles, even though we know they are not there. This is an adaptation of a well-known study by Bradley and Petry (1977). Gestalt psychologists would say that our perception is determined by

Figure 2.1 *Illustrations of Gestalt principles*

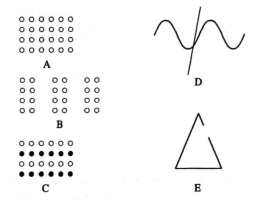

Figure 2.2 *Gestalt illustration*

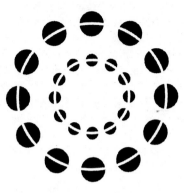

the context in which we find objects, and demonstrates how the whole influences the perception of the parts.

There are of course other explanations for these perceptual phenomena, but the Gestalt explanation is very attractive – that we will always tend to perceive things in their simplest, most unified form. This is known as the simplicity principle, and can be applied to thinking and problem solving too. Thorndike's explanation for learning to solve problems was that trial and error would lead to associations. Gestalt theorists claim that animals (and humans) develop insight – the experience of what has to be done to achieve a goal. These ideas of the Gestaltists are still influential, but are not as popular in modern psychology as they previously were. The next sections will examine the ideas that have been developed and researched in the second half of this century.

Information Processing

The idea that information is taken into the human system and transformed through a variety of processes is an attractive one. It is clear and allows us to visualise what may be happening in our own minds. Information processing as a psychological perspective was not introduced until the 1960s, but there were various approaches that can be regarded as the harbingers of such ideas.

Mental Chronometry

In the 19th century, researchers such as Helmholtz were interested in the reflex arc (the things that have actions such as making your knee jerk when hit with something). Behaviourists would simply say that the stimulus (the bang from the mallet) has made the organism (you) respond (jerk). But this does not satisfy some people, and they want to measure the speed of responses. Helmholtz came up with the subtraction method in order to determine the speed of transmission along the nerve pathways. He measured the reaction time for response of a muscle in a frog's leg to electric shock. He measured when the source of the shock was close to the muscle that was contracting, and also when distant. The difference between these, he divided by the distance and got an estimate of the speed of nerve conduction. Donders saw the logic of this method, and applied it to mental operations. His participants reacted to a stimulus as quickly as possible, and this reaction time was measured. However, he broke down this reaction time into several other pieces. Between the start of the stimulus and the actual reaction is the detection time – when there is only one stimulus. In another case, participants react to one of two stimuli, by choosing perhaps which key to press. This is the choice reaction time. Donders wanted the decision time, so subtracted detection time from choice reaction time. He argued that choice reaction time is a result of two mental processes, detection and decision, and this happens in every type of task. This might not be strictly true, but it is an interesting type of estimation, and it was very common to see this chronometric method being used to investigate mental operations. The problem here is that mental chronometry still does not get at the details of the cognitive operations, but simply at the patterns associating stimulus and response.

Human Performance Research

An alternative approach to studying human functioning is also through measuring performance, but with the objective of designing equipment such that it fits the human operator to optimal requirements. This is now one of the best known areas of applied psychology, and came to prominence during World War II. A particular area of performance studied was the reading of instrumentation in aircraft, together with performance in emergencies, etc. Research carried out during the war and in the following few years led to determining the best kind of displays for reading information quickly and accurately, and this was applied to various other fields, such as automobile design.

Human factors research, as it is known, uses a model very much like that found in behaviourism, but from the human point of view. Humans as communication channels could become overloaded, but the idea of information selection that grew out of this work is very influential. Psychology has therefore had a great effect on the design and use of machinery. Conversely, as we will see in the next section, machinery has influenced psychology.

Computer Simulation

Developments in technology have affected just about every aspect of our lives. Theoretical psychology is not immune from this, and the architecture of the computer lends itself to the use of analogy and metaphor in very fruitful ways. The similarity between the ways in which humans deal with information and the action of the serial computer is too good to miss. If humans process symbols when solving problems, the fact that computers do this too means we can use the computer as a model of ourselves. Fundamental differences between human and machine must be remembered, of course, and we should be clear that this is simply a metaphor, a peg on which to hang ideas. This functionalist representation of ourselves has been very useful in Cognitive Psychology. In memory research, for example, the form that computer architecture takes allowed the development of several models which could be tested.

The other advantage of the computer in psychology is the use of simulation. Once a theoretical model has been constructed, the computer simulation of it can actually allow the testing. If any discrepancy between the model's performance and the theory is observed, then work is needed to bring the two closer together. This work indicates aspects about the human and computer performance that may be novel. The use of modelling, simulation and analogy in this way means that we can use the machine metaphor to explore our own cognitive functioning. We think of the computer as an information processor, which means we can examine ourselves in the same way. This is the fundamental element of the information processing approach, and one which we will return to several times.

The Information Processing Approach

The information processing approach to studying human cognition is therefore a relatively modern idea based on well-established antecedents. There are several models of the links between cognitive functions that theorists in the area have proposed. Many of these models suggest that physical stimuli are drawn into the systems and changed into a form that can be utilised (transduction). Then there is some form of sensory storage, followed by pattern recognition. These pieces of information are now in a form ready for processing in short term or working memory, to be again transformed or encoded for long term storage. Long term storage is highly organised so that retrieval is maximised, together with usage for problem solving and expertise.

Variations on this model form the basis of the information processing approach, but it does have problems. Broadbent (1984) suggests that this simple model is too linear: information moves in one direction, whereas there may be interaction and counterflow. There may also be high levels of individual differences, not accounted for in the models. McClelland (1981) also suggested that one process may start before another has finished: they may *cascade*. So whilst the next few chapters present theories and research in such a way as to suggest a fairly simple route, do not forget that it may not be quite so linear.

One theory that grew out of this thinking was connectionism. Similar in many ways to associationism, connectionism stresses the importance of the strength of links between material. It also examines the possibility of *parallel processing* (many connections working at the same time) and mediation between information in and information out. We will examine this approach later in the book.

Artificial Intelligence

One final area to consider in relation to Cognitive Psychology is that of Artificial Intelligence. This is an area of study bringing together psychology and computer science. It is an endeavour to fully understand the nature of human cognition, in order to build machine intelligence. Turing (1950) stated that there were certain criteria under which we will be able to test whether or not we have intelligent machines. We will examine these ideas later, but we aware that there is a great deal going on in cognitive science that the mainly historical perspective of this book might not make clear.

Self-test Questions

1 What is the perceptual threshold?
2 How are associations formed?
3 Why do spoonerisms fail to support the behaviourist tradition?
4 In what ways can the simplicity principle be applied?
5 How is decision time calculated?
6 Has psychology influenced the design and use of machinery, or have the machines influenced the study of human cognition?
7 What are the three major problems with a traditional information processing approach?

Information Gathering

This part is concerned with how information reaches the cognitive system and what happens to it in the initial stages. Chapter 3 follows information through initial sensation to the process of perception, and Chapter 4 looks at theories and research on how information is selected for attention. Once selected, we become aware of it, so our consciousness is examined in Chapter 5.

CHAPTER 3

The Sensational Perceptual System

Key terms

computational theory a theory suggesting that vision is a series of computable steps

constructivist theory a theory suggesting that perception is the matching of input and stored memories, resulting in an amalgam of both

direct perception a theory which supposes that all that is required for accurate perception is the sensory input, a data-driven theory

pattern recognition the identification of recurring combinations of environmental inputs

threshold the point at which stimuli can be detected (absolute) or the difference between two stimuli can be detected (differential)

transduction the process of converting energy at the sensory receptive field into neural impulses

visual acuity the extent of the ability to see fine detail

visual cortex the area of the brain sensitive to visual input; there are also areas known to be receptive to auditory, olfactory, gustatory, somatosensory and proprioceptive input

Key names

Campbell and Robson • Carlson • Gandevia, McCloskey and Burke • Gibson • Gregory • Hubel and Wiesel • Marr • McClelland and Rumelhart • Sekuler and Blake

Sensation and perception are the mechanisms by which we gather information about the world, and begin the processing of that information. It is important to study how we do this for several reasons. The world is a complicated place, and by all accounts becoming more complicated. As cognitivists, we need to know what it is about the environment, and the detection of stimuli, that can enhance or impair cognitive function. In order to tailor the world to humans, we need to know how devices should be designed, and designed to fit with the sensory and perceptual system.

We can assume that cognitive phenomena are affected by, and are a result of events happening in the world, so studying the identification and processing of sensory signals may provide clues to how 'higher-order' cognitions work. Also detection of signals may be affected by experience and needs. So we will examine perception as a pathway from the raw detection of sensory input to the complex matter of pattern recognition.

Sensation

The first point of contact between our own inner personal world and external reality is through our sensory system – the point at which sensation becomes perception. In the last chapter, we looked at one way of studying this relationship, psychophysics. Fechner's study of perceptual thresholds has added much to our understanding of sensation. Let us look at this area in a little more detail.

Sensory Systems

There is a particular progress of stimuli from the outside world to the inner. The stimulus affects a receptor by changing energy, which converts (*transduces*) into neural impulses, transmitting the information to the cortical structures designed to interpret it. This progress is the same in any sensory modality, each of which has been studied to different extents in psychology. The major ones examined are vision and hearing.

visual acuity the level at which fine detail in images can be detected. Measurement is commonly by presentation of black and white stripes (gratings) of progressively reduced width, until the acuity threshold is reached. The thresholds that are measured via gratings are expressed in terms of cycles per degree. Another measure of acuity is expressed in terms of the distance at which objects, usually letters, which produce images on the retina of 0.005 mm can be detected. If an individual is standing 20 feet from the letter chart, and can see letters that the average person can see, then they have 20/20 vision. Needing to stand at 20 feet to see letters the average person can see at 30 feet is 20/30 vision

Vision

The eye is constructed so that light reflected from an object will fall on the retina. The receptors in the retina are *rods* and *cones*. Rods are very sensitive to light, but insensitive to colour, whereas cones are involved in colour vision. The light is focused onto the retina via the lens, changes in which are known as accommodation. Abnormalities can affect accommodation, which affects *visual acuity*.

Once light is detected it triggers certain chemical reactions that excite neural pathways associated with areas in the eye. From there they pass into the optic nerve and hence to the visual cortex. Hubel and Wiesel (1979), in their work in recording single cell firing in the brain, discovered *feature detectors*. These are neurones that fire only when stimulation matches a particular pattern. They found that there are *simple* cells that respond to lines in specific orientation and location in the visual field, *complex* cells that respond to more of the visual field, and possibly motion, and *hypercomplex* cells that respond to size. There are other feature detectors for colour, contrast and texture (Livingstone and Hubel, 1988).

The detection of light and images, then, is transferred to the brain, in which detection is highly specialised. The translation and interpretation of these excitations are visual perception.

Hearing

Sound is composed of waves and is measured in several ways. The *frequency* of a sound is the measure of how many times the wave cycles or how often the wave expands and contracts. Hertz (Hz) are wave cycles per second; the higher the Hz, the higher is the tone we hear. An orchestra tunes to a note called concert A, which is 440 Hz. An octave above that is 880 Hz. The normal range of young adult human hearing is 15 to 20 000 Hz, but this diminishes with age. Human voices range from 100 to 3500 Hz, but again this diminishes with age, as any old soprano will demonstrate!

Sounds are not composed of one frequency, though, and the other aspect of sound is its *complexity.* Multiple frequencies give us the psychological property of *timbre* or sound texture. This is what gives a voice its unique properties. In addition to technical ability, we can recognise our favourite singer from the timbre of the voice. A note of the same frequency played on a piano will sound completely different played on a flute. The sequence of sounds in particular temporal order is recognised as music – well, sometimes – depending on age, culture and preference, and also the *amplitude* of sounds. The amplitude gives us the perception of loudness, and is the height and depth of the wave. Amplitude is measured in decibels (dB), normal conversation being around 50–60 dB. Prolonged exposure to sounds over 90 dB can cause permanent hearing loss. With rock concerts often being played at up to 130 dB, the pain threshold, your parents are right – that music *is* painful!

The sound receptors are in the middle and inner ear. The outer ear is simply a collection and magnification point; the middle ear converts the air pressure into movement of tiny bones, which is transduced in the inner ear to waves in fluid that generate the neural signals. The auditory nerve then transmits these signals to the brain. However, some of the information also reaches the reticular activating formation, which explains the function of sound in arousal (see Chapter 5). You will wake up in response to changes in sound more often than to changes in light.

The auditory cortex has specific sections that respond to different frequencies, much as the visual cortex has specific feature detectors. There is also more devoted to mid-spectrum frequencies than to sounds heard less often (Sekular and Blake, 1994). Neurones can also respond to 'movement' in sound (frequency changes) and spatial location. However, unlike motion and location in visual space, sounds are located by loudness (indicating closeness) and by the differential speed of hearing by each ear. Sound moves more slowly than light, and there will be a perceived difference in hearing in the right and left ear, when the sound is coming from a particular direction.

Other Senses

Vision and hearing have been studied more extensively than other senses because they are more highly developed in humans. There are four other senses that serve important functions.

Smell

The olfactory sense can detect danger, discriminates unpalatable food from palatable, and aids in recognition of others. In animals other than humans, smell regulates sexual behaviour, due to the production of scent messages known as *pheromones*. There is some very limited evidence that there are olfactory cues for reproduction in humans, such as gender identification, and the synchronisation of menstrual cycles in women living together. So much for perfume!

Molecules of substances in the air are detected by the smell receptors in the nasal cavities. Transduction takes place in the olfactory epithelium, which holds the olfactory receptors. Humans have about 10 million receptors, but dogs have 200 million, so it is obvious which animal is known for its ability to track by scent. The olfactory nerve transmits the neural signals via the olfactory bulb to the olfactory cortex. Unlike other senses, there is direct transmission, but the olfactory cortex has links to other brain structures, particularly those associated with emotion and with taste.

Taste

Whereas smell is the detection of air molecules, taste, the gustatory sense, is the detection of molecules soluble in saliva. Taste and smell are very closely linked; molecules from chewed food will pass into the nasal cavities, and the olfactory sensation actually forms a major part of taste.

Both taste and smell are involved in survival, in that toxic substances will taste 'bad' (bitter) and substances that provide energy taste 'good' (sweet). This differentiation between good and bad tastes holds no matter what culture is examined, and no matter at what age the different tastes are presented.

Transduction happens in the taste buds, which is very early in the sensory process. Each taste bud contains 50–150 receptor cells, which are constantly being replaced as they wear out due to frequent contact (Margolskee, 1995). What is not known is whether they are replaced more quickly in habitual over-eaters. Neural signals are sent, via the cranial nerves, to the hind-brain and from there either to the thalamus and the gustatory cortex, which detect taste, or to the limbic system. The latter pathway is the one that allows the immediate behavioural response to taste, such as spitting out bad tasting substances.

Skin

The skin is sensitive to pressure and temperature and receptors send information to the spinal cord. In this way contact can be made with motor neurones allowing reflexive action, such as moving away from hot surfaces. Pressure receptors also send information to the somatosensory cortex, in which the sensations from the hands are represented by very high acuity. Temperature receptors are sensitive to either cold or warmth.

Proprioceptive sense

We can also detect body position and movement, and location of self in space. *Kinaesthesia* is the information about relative movement and position of the body and limbs. Receptors are in the joints, transducing information about position of bones, and also in the tendons and muscles, transducing information about muscle tension related to body position (Gandevia *et al.*, 1992).

The other proprioceptive sense, for location in space, is the *vestibular* sense. This provides information about gravity and movement. These sense organs are in the ear: the semicircular canals and vestibular sacs transduce signals about relative movement and gravitational pull, possibly to the cerebellum, and a region of the temporal cortex (Carlson, 1991).

Perception

The process of perception is two-fold. Sensory information is provided by external stimuli and accessed by the sense organs, and stored information is used to make sense of the world. There are several theories about the contribution of both in the perceptual process.

Gibson's Theory of Direct Perception

Gibson (1979) argued that sensory information is the more important in the perceptual process. His original work looked at the problems associated with landing aircraft. When approaching the landing strip, pilots experience a visual illusion associated with optic flow patterns. This means that the point towards which the pilot is moving appears motionless, but the rest of the visual environment appears to move away from that point. This is known as a constant aspect approach. Thus the information available provides the pilot with unambiguous information about the approach. Gibson rejected the idea that we attach meaning to stimuli by relating them to stored knowledge, and

Figure 3.1 *The visual cliff*

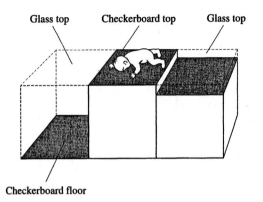

said that the information needed to act in the environment is wholly contained within the objects there, and we need nothing else to function perceptually. Hence the theory is termed *direct perception.* The sensory information is so rich and detailed we need nothing else. Gibson used the laboratory studies on the *visual cliff* to provide evidence for this theory.

> **visual cliff** a table which has half set with a 'shallow' checkerboard (solid), the other half a 'deep' checkerboard, which appears to fall away sharply, but is in fact covered with glass – see Figure 3.1

Babies will not crawl onto the 'drop' side of the visual cliff, even when they have no experience of precipices. Gibson says this is because depth cues, and avoidance of drops, are innate endowments.

When perception is accurate, this theory gives an adequate explanation, but fails to account for errors. Other theorists suggest alternatives to Gibson.

Constructive Theories

Gregory (1972) argued that perceptions are constructions from pieces of sensory data and pieces of information from the memory, which are themselves constructions. Errors and inadequacies in perception are explained, in that stimulus information may be itself inadequate, and bring about an erroneous construction.

Neisser (1967, 1976) went even further and proposed that perception involves *schemata, exploration* and *stimuli.* Perceptual schemata (internal representations) direct perceptual exploration towards relevant environmental stimuli: see Figure 3.2. Exploration may mean moving around, and allows sampling of the available stimuli. If the samples do not match the schema, then the schema may be modified. If the perceptual stimuli are of poor quality, then the schemata play a larger part. Such constructivist theories can explain visual illusion better than direct perception theories. If

Figure 3.2 *Neisser's perception model*

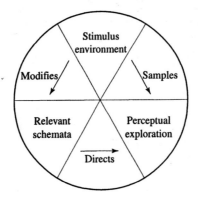

Figure 3.3 *The Müller–Leyer illusion*

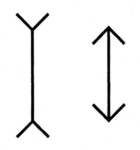

the stored information is being used to make sense of current stimuli, the illusion may be the result of applying this knowledge incorrectly.

Gregory explained the Müller–Leyer illusion (see Figure 3.3) by the left line being interpreted as the inside corner of a room, and the right line being the outside corner of a building. In other words, we are seeing the left line as having fins that are receding from us and the line is perceived as further away. We perceive objects as being the same size even if they are distant from each other, i.e. we know that two people are the same size, even though one is close to us, and the other is far away. This is known as *size constancy* and Gregory suggested that this is what is being misapplied in the Müller–Leyer illusion. There are difficulties with this explanation, and it is possible that there are several factors involved in illusions.

Computational Theories

Another alternative theory has been proposed through the attempts to simulate human processes on computers. Marr (1982) suggests that visual perception is a series of stages of successively more complexity. This theory is explored in more detail in Chapter 17. Marr's attempts to implement the theoretical model onto a computer were only partially successful, suggesting even more complexity in visual perception than was thought.

This complexity is probably due to *all* the theories being partially correct.

Thresholds

Much of the psychological experimentation in sensation and perception has concerned the perceptual thresholds. Absolute thresholds are the levels of least intensity needed to detect a stimulus. Such thresholds vary from individual to individual, and between situations. For example, the absolute threshold of sound is that most people can hear the ticking of a watch at 20 feet, but cannot hear the same watch when interfering noise is present. Such distraction can be internal, such as random firing of neurones, and psychological states such as fatigue (Harder *et al.*, 1989), and is known as *noise* even in modalities other than hearing. The detection of stimuli against background noise is known as *signal detection* (Swets, 1992), suggesting that sensation and perception are not passive, but that we make judgements about the presence of signals. Experiments in which signals are presented with or without noise, and in which the signals may be present or absent, show some interesting differences in perception. Participants may report a stimulus when none is present, or miss some. Noise alone can lead some participants to report a signal's presence. This difference in threshold for reporting signal presence depends on many psychological factors such as expectation and motivation.

Development

New-born babies have relatively poor visual perception. Adults can perceive shades of grey that have contrast values of less than 1%, whereas a baby's threshold of detectability is about 30%, with poor visual acuity (detected by the visual preference method). Adult levels are reached at about 6 months old, and it is at this stage that babies appear to start recognising faces. There does appear to be some colour vision in the new-born, however (Adams *et al.*, 1986), with discrimination between green, yellow, red and grey, but not grey and blue. Babies also actively seek stimulation, by shifting eye direction, and they prefer moving stimuli to stationary (Slater, 1989).

As such it can be seen that new-born babies have immature visual systems, but that the maturation is rapid. This development appears to depend on experience, coupled with biological state. Adults born blind, but who have gained sight via surgical procedures, report difficulty with interpreting visual stimuli, and do not always develop full perceptual skill. Animals reared in the dark have much poorer visual ability than others, with accompanying lack of development in the visual system. Such evidence suggests that there is some basic biological basis for vision, mediated by experience with the environment.

Other senses demonstrate a different pattern of development. Taste appears to be fully developed at birth – a baby is fully equipped with taste buds, and can distinguish between the four primary taste sensations. Likewise with smell, babies will distinguish between their own mother and another woman in the same stage of lactation, by smell alone (Macfarlane, 1975).

Despite being unable to make coherent sounds, babies will also discriminate between speech sounds, suggesting an innate disposition to orient towards human speech.

It would appear then that all senses are functioning from birth, but that none operate at adult levels. Sophistication of perception is achieved very quickly, however, with infants able to discriminate various elements of the environment very successfully. The evidence suggests that there is innate, or congenital, ability which develops under influence from interaction with the environment. Neonates are predisposed to this interaction.

Organisation

The information that arrives at our sensory organs is, as James (1890) described, 'a buzzing, booming confusion'. Our perceptual system makes sense of this by integrating sensation into meaningful units called *percepts*. This means putting them into shapes and patterns (*form perception*), three-dimensional figures (*depth perception*), and stable images (*perceptual constancy*).

Form perception

We have already considered (Chapter 2) the Gestaltist interpretation of perception. Gestalt ideas would say that perception is more than simply the sum of the sensations we receive, and that there are several rules by which sensory input is transformed into meaningful perception.

We inherently discriminate between the item we view, and its background. This rule is known as *figure–ground perception*, and anomalies in it show how it works. There are various pictures in which you can see one figure or another, and with a bit of staring your perception can change from one to the other quite quickly. The retinal image, however, remains constant, but we see one part of it as figure and the other as ground. This applies in other modalities too: smell a delicious perfume, and all other scents blend into background smell.

Other rules include *similarity* (grouping similar elements within the perceptual field) and *proximity* (grouping items that are close to each other). The principle of *good continuation* means that we organise stimuli so that they appear to be continuous lines or patterns. Figure 3.4 appears to have a white triangle in the middle, but it is not really there; we make the lines continuous via perceptual processes.

Figure 3.4 *Illustration of the principle of good continuation*

The *simplicity* principle states that we perceive the simplest pattern possible, and *closure* means we perceive incomplete objects as complete.

The Gestalt approach has identified important principles, but does not attempt to account for the origin of those principles. In particular, the neural aspects of perception are not explained by simply enumerating principles and phenomena. An alternative to this theory is that proposed by Campbell and Robson (1968). They suggested that there are multiple channels that activate the various receptive fields at once, but that the *function* of the perception determines the level of activation. In other words, if we need to view high detail in an image then the appropriate neurones are activated in comparison to when we need to view the whole picture, as an overview (Field, 1987).

Depth perception
Visual input is integrated from both eyes to give *binocular cues*. The visual cortex is made up mostly of binocular cells, receiving input from both eyes, and some of these respond to the disparities between the images given from each eye, giving depth perception. Together with these cues there are sensations from the movement of the lenses in the eyes, which give information about relative distance.

There are similar responses in other sensory modalities, which allow us to interpret our three-dimensional world.

Perceptual constancy
We see images and their positions as relatively stable. If a box is moved around in front of our eyes, the shape of the retinal image changes, but we know that the box remains the same shape and size. Likewise if we change the illumination on an object, we still perceive the same colour. Look at snow-covered fields at twilight, and they are still white, and a black cat in sunlight is still a black cat. Shape, size and colour constancy all suggest that there is a high level of organisation in the perceptual system, as do form perception and depth perception.

Perceptual interpretation is the point at which sensation and memory interact. The various theories of perception suggest different levels of contribution from experience. It is most likely that there is an interaction between bottom-up, data-driven processes (as suggested by theories of direct perception) and top-down constructivist processes. One area where this interaction is most apparent is in pattern recognition.

Pattern Recognition

We assign meaning to objects in the world by recognising them. This appears to be an unconscious process; the identification of objects 'simply happens'. But in order to recognise an object we must have seen it, or something matching it, previously. Not only that, but we can identify items as belonging to a particular class of objects, even though they may bear no apparent relationship to the members of the class we have already encountered. For example, suppose you had never seen a Great Dane. Chances are you would still say it was a dog. Pattern recognition is obviously a process of matching stimulus to long term store. There are several theories that attempt to account for this.

Template theories fall down because they suppose exact matches are stored in order to recognise stimuli. Variations on these theories suggest that input is pre-processed in order to 'normalise' position, size, etc., but it is unclear how this might happen, and there is little evidence to support such ideas.

Feature analysis theories suppose that complex patterns are broken down into their component features, and that these are compared to stored *prototypes* (typical instances). A prototype is the pattern derived from averaging all examples encountered. The instances that have been experienced are broken down into features, an average of each feature is taken across all the examples, then the pattern is built from these averages. There is some evidence supporting this: the Hubel and Wiesel work on the visual cortex suggested that feature detectors do work on single items, putting all the features together. There is also some support from studies of language, which appears to be a process of breaking input down into important units in a hierarchy of features (see McClelland and Rumelhart, 1981, for more details).

The problem with feature analysis theories is the difficulty of specifying adequate feature sets for complex patterns, and when changing context and purpose. Also components of items do not necessarily give us the possibility of predicting the experience derived from the whole pattern (Pomerantz, 1985). There is also no way to account for the relationship between items.

It is likely that connectionist theories have a better explanation, and are more flexible. Stressing the element of learning in pattern perception, connectionist, or parallel distributed processing (p.d.p.) theories offer a more adaptable model of perception. These suggest that instead of features being analysed and stored, inputs will excite or inhibit neural pathways, evoking a pattern, in order to discriminate between it and others stored in similar ways.

Summary

The first part of our cognitive system, then, is the contact with the outside world through our sensory system. However, until the sensations excite the neural receptors in the central nervous system, we are not using truly cognitive processes. Perception is the psychological process by which we understand and make sense of sensation. The next point in the chain is the selection of these sensory inputs that we have perceived, for further processing. The next two chapters will explore the way in which this happens.

Self-test Questions

1 Write down the process from detection of stimuli by the sense organs to detection in the brain, in vision, hearing and taste.
2 How do direct theories of perception differ from constructivist theories?
3 What can babies see?
4 What evidence is there to support the idea that perception is organised?

CHAPTER 4

Attention and Selection

Key terms

attenuation tuning down information rather than filtering it out

automaticity when a process becomes so familiar one no longer needs to pay attention to it

bottleneck theories models of selective attention in which information must pass through an area where there is insufficient space for everything

capacity models models of attention in which selection is carried out on the basis of resources rather than filters

cocktail party phenomenon a situation where filtering is seen quite clearly, but also demonstrates that salient information will be processed

dichotic listening a way of studying auditory stimuli processing

filter models channels of limited capacity in bottleneck theories

late selection models theories of attention in which selection of material is made in short term rather than sensory memory

Key names

Broadbent • Cherry • Deutsch and Deutsch • Kahneman • Neisser • Posner • Schnieder and Shiffrin • Treisman

The study of attention is the study of how information is selected from all that is presented to the human sensory and perceptual system. It appears that there is a limited capacity to deal with all the information we receive, and that there are cognitive processes involved in selecting stimuli for attention. These stimuli are not selected on the basis of loudness or brightness or indeed importance. For example, how many of you will remain listening to a lecture when there is something much more interesting happening outside the window? The study of attention, therefore, is important as the first point of the internal system that brings a cognitive process to bear on information. Research in attention attempts to define this area, then concentrates on models of selective attention and processing capacity, automatic processing of information, consciousness and the neurology of attention. We will examine each of these in turn.

Definitions of Attention

We all think we know what we mean by attention. James (1890) declared:

> Every one knows what attention is. It is the taking possession by the mind, in a clear and vivid form, of one out of what seem several simultaneously possible objects or trains of thought.

Attention appears to be the action of concentrating and focusing mental effort. This only holds true for the conscious act of attending, however. We can actually attend to other things without being completely conscious of them, for example, talking to friends whilst walking. The conversation is taking conscious attention, but it would be a problem if it took all of the mental effort. There are two different types of studies which allow us to examine how attention happens: the selective attention which is used to choose the stimuli on which we concentrate, and divided attention when several things are done simultaneously.

Selective Attention

Selective attention, sometimes referred to as 'focused attention', is the study of how participants perform when asked to concentrate on particular stimuli. Early work was carried out in the area of auditory stimuli, and led to the development of several models of attention.

Models of Attention

There are two major theories of how the system for attention is organised. These come under the general headings of 'bottleneck' and 'filter' models.

Bottleneck Theories

dichotic listening is a particular type of study set up in a laboratory in which participants hear different stimuli in each ear. Often participants are requested to attend to only one stimulus type, or to only one ear. The way in which it can be checked that they are doing this is by asking them to shadow, to repeat what they are hearing in that ear

In 1953 Cherry made a discovery during a study on dichotic listening, in which participants attended to one ear (ensured by shadowing).

Participants had no problem with shadowing properly, but could also report items concerning the secondary message, such as the physical and acoustic characteristics. However, they could not tell the meaning of this message or the content, and could not detect the language or recognise words from the message. This is often referred to as the cocktail party phenomenon. This is not a suggestion that Cherry went to a lot of cocktail parties, but it refers to the fact that we can attend to one conversation even when many people are speaking at once, i.e. we can filter out a great deal of the stimuli presented to us, but we are still attending at some level, because part of the message gets through. Imagine being at a party listening to a riveting conversation with a delightful person you have only just met, when someone else shouts your name. You might want to filter it out, but it gets through. However, what you can filter is the fact that a drunken partygoer has just spilt his drink down your brand new clothes (until you get home, that is).

Filters

Broadbent developed a theory that attempted to account for this. Not the fact that if someone has drink spilt over them it's bound to be you (that's probability theory), but the idea that we can filter out unnecessary information.

Broadbent envisaged that the focus of attention is determined by a filter – a channel of limited capacity – and a detection device. These are preceded by a sensory register, essentially an area of memory for stimuli recently presented. This latter is thought to be extremely short in duration, but an exact representation of stimuli in each sensory modality. According to Neisser (1967), these stimuli are subjected to a pre-attentive analysis identifying physical characteristics, and determining whether or not they will undergo further processing after the selective filter. Figure 4.1 shows the pathways in Broadbent's model.

Having a limited capacity filter has implications when one is asked to do two tasks simultaneously. Broadbent suggested that the filter switches between channels in the sensory register, transferring as much as it can to the limited channel. Hence the name bottleneck: a lot of information passes into the register, but cannot get through the channel. Think of pouring wine back into a bottle (as if you ever would!). If your jug holds a lot of wine, and you try to pour it all back in too quickly, the narrow neck would cause the wine to run down the side, and you would lose some. The sensory register in this case is a parallel element, many things held together, and it tries to pass them

Figure 4.1 *Broadbent's model of selective attention*

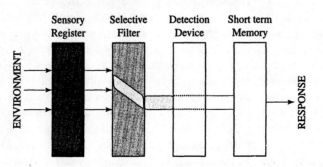

all to a serial channel, which can only handle one thing at a time, so some information is lost. If the information reaches the detection device it is analysed for meaning, and it is at this point we become conscious of it.

So does this account for the cocktail party phenomenon described by Cherry? Information from two sources will be received by the sensory register, and receive pre-attentive analysis for physical characteristics, but only some will receive further analysis. However, we can see that some information will get through from the secondary source, and Broadbent's theory does not take into account the finding of Moray (1959) which confirms what happened when someone attracted your attention at the party. His participants did recognise their names in the secondary source. So Broadbent can explain the filtering of information, but not the fact that salient information will get through. Treisman, in 1960, also discovered that the meaning of the message in the non-shadowed ear could get through. She also showed that semantic content was actually analysed very early in the system. If you give the participants identical messages in each ear, but play them asynchronously (one slightly behind the other), the two are identified as the same, but there are critical timing differences. This led Treisman to modify Broadbent's theory.

Attenuation

Incoming stimuli undergo three different types of analysis or test. Think of a sound passing to the system.

1 It is identified in terms of pitch, frequency and intensity. It undergoes an acoustic, or more generally a physical analysis.
2 It is examined for type (is it a linguistic sound? can it be grouped into syllables, words, etc.?) This is a syntactic analysis.
3 Finally we might recognise words and meanings when it has been subjected to a semantic analysis.

Test 1 disentangles male voices from female, for example, but at this point the sound will not receive any semantic analysis because it does not require attention to distinguish lower and higher voices. Treisman therefore said that the non-shadowed message in dichotic listening is not tuned out or filtered, but tuned down, or *attenuated*. Her model is different because Broadbent's appears to show that pre-attentive analysis is crude and physical, whereas attenuation is much more complex, even to the point of including a semantic analysis. The Broadbent filter is all or nothing, whereas attenuation suggests that non-selected channels are simply tuned down. This gives a good account of many things that researchers have noted. Unfortunately it is far too complex. This causes problems, not just for psychology students trying to understand it, but because it doesn't make cognitive sense. Pre-attentive analysis here is almost as complete as full attention, so what's the point?

Something much simpler was postulated by Deutsch and Deutsch in 1963. They said that all incoming stimuli are passed for processing, and

Figure 4.2 *Deutsch and Deutsch's model of selective attention*

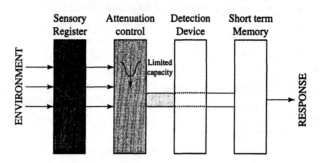

selection is made in an area known as working memory, a short term store (Figure 4.2). We will examine working memory theories later in the book, but for now all we need to know is that it is an area of highly active storage. This suggests that selection is very late in the process.

Late Selection
Participants should recognise information even when it is presented to a non-shadowed ear. Lewis in 1970 tested this in the normal dichotic listening set-up, with words in both ears. Some words presented to each were semantically unrelated, and some were synonyms. As participants repeated shadowed words, there was a delay when the non-shadowed word was a synonym, but not for the unrelated words. Broadbent's model would say that the non-shadowed ear is tuned out and there should be no difference in response time; Treisman's model would suggest that tuning down should stop the semantic relationship affecting response. Neither can explain Lewis's findings.

So how does late selection work? Transmission is of all material in parallel into the working memory. The capacity of this area is limited, and so only some material can be stored. Judgements are made about the material's importance and important bits are given elaborated analysis. This gives it a more durable representation. Importance is determined due to working memory being 'pre-set' by the task in hand.

So we now have a picture of attention as, crudely, a funnel, but this might be misleading. Later studies suggested that it might be more helpful to think of it as a spotlight with a controllable lens. This might give a very tight beam (a high level of sensitivity) or a wider one. The next models we will examine will see what to make of that idea.

Capacity Models

Kahneman (1973) suggested that we should not be worried about where or what the bottleneck is, but what exactly is going on when a person is carrying

KAHNEMAN (1973)

out a task. He said that simultaneous tasks can be performed in *optimum* conditions, but if one task demands more attention the other loses out, as when listening to a lecture and writing down its content in shorthand. A difficult concept may demand more concentration so it does not get written down very well. That is why you cannot understand your notes when you get home, not because the lecturer is not very good.

So Kahneman suggested that rather than a limited channel, we have a resource allocation unit or policy that controls how you use limited resources. Several complex stimuli can use up resources quickly and additional stimuli or feedback lose out on attention. But there are stages in which resources are allocated specifically to process incoming stimuli, and this is under our cognitive control.

enduring dispositions are the tendency to pay attention to loud noises, flashes, your name being spoken, etc.
momentary intentions are situational dispositions

The number of resources may also be flexible. This is determined at any one time by arousal level, rising up to a certain point. Stimuli are accorded resources via an allocation policy, affected by *enduring dispositions* and *momentary intentions*.

Anderson *et al.* (1987) showed how these dispositions are related, using the 'attentional inertia' of children watching TV. Attentional inertia is the tendency to continue processing the primary source the longer the attention is on it. When children watch TV, they get completely wrapped up in it. This study is about what happens as they watch for longer and longer periods. At various times a distractor stimulus was given, and in order to pay attention to it the children had to turn their heads. Anderson *et al.* found that the longer the periods of TV gazing, the more likely they were to continue watching, despite something distracting going on elsewhere. The psychologists interpreted this as 'attentional inertia' in that processing is more likely to continue in the primary sources because it requires more and more of the resources to be allocated to it. The momentary intentions (watching TV) are influencing the allocation policy, so fewer resources are available for enduring dispositions (distraction). If the distractor had been an extremely loud bang, arousal level would have gone up and the enduring dispositions would have come into play. So this is why you don't notice the chip pan burning when there's a very interesting film to watch, at least until you start choking in the smoke and a fear response is needed.

So this model (Figure 4.3) suggests a cognitive capacity system with the following predictions:

1 Competing sources of stimuli produce non-specific interference – doing two things at once does not lead to interference, but they do compete for limited resources, therefore we can do two things at once as long as we don't exceed the available resources.

2 When total processing demands exceed capacity, performance on one task will suffer when we add another.

Figure 4.3 *Capacity model of selective attention*

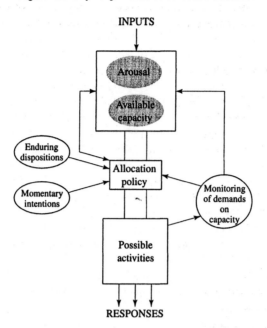

3 The allocation policy is flexible and can be altered to suit the demand of incoming stimuli.

Let's examine these predictions. In 1971 Posner and Boies asked participants to do two tasks, letter matching and tapping. They were asked to pay full attention to letter matching. They were given a visual warning signal and shown one letter for 50 ms after the signal. Then another letter appeared 1 second later and they had to indicate whether the letters matched by typing 'y' or 'n' with their right hand. In addition to this, participants were asked to tap with the left hand when they heard an auditory signal presented through headphones they were wearing. The findings were significant differences in the response time depending on when the auditory signal was given. If the sound was played before the visual signal, then response time was short, but increased when the sound was later. This supports predictions 1 and 2. We can process competing stimuli when capacity is not used up. When activities compete, such as retrieving the first letter and comparing it, processing on other tasks loses out.

Prediction number 3, on the other hand, is supported by a study in 1978 by Johnston and Heinz in which participants were asked to shadow messages which were either high or low physical discriminability from the non-shadowed message (male and female voices usually have high physical discriminability) or had semantic differences, or both. At the same time participants responded to changes in the intensity of a light. When the messages had physical differences, participants responded to the secondary task better, regardless of semantic differences. So when using the minimum analysis that is necessary, we can allocate resources as needed.

Evaluation of Models

So, bottleneck theories suggest that stimuli compete for space, and interfere with each other; capacity models suggest that as long as sufficient resources are available, processing can take place. What is clear is that we cannot process all of the information that we receive. Attenuation seems to account for most of the research findings, but still seems far too complex to be the ideal. Perhaps a combination of the two sets of models will prove to be the case. Such models, and the research findings associated with them, suggest that processing capacity is limited, for whatever reason. This might be limitation of resources, or limitation of input capacity, or both. What is interesting is the fact that any information gets through at all from the multiplicity of stimuli we receive. There are two interesting points to consider in the light of this. The first is that we can do several things at once, and indicate that attention can be divided. The second is tasks that we carry out frequently. This is referred to as automatic processing.

Divided Attention

It is true that sometimes attention must be focused, and the incoming stimuli must be selected, but we can also do several things at once. The restrictions on this appear to be what those things are. The difficulty and familiarity of tasks are the limitations here. Most people can walk and talk, although apparently some American presidents have difficulty walking and chewing gum. The difficulty of tasks is also not a function of each one separately, but the mental effort required to combine the two. It may not be too difficult to read this book, and it may not be too demanding to write a letter, but both together? I think not. The amount of familiarity you have with a task is also a limitation on attention. Learning to drive a car is quite difficult at first, and there is no way you would want your friend in the back seat telling you about this great book on Cognitive Psychology she has just read, but a year after you have passed your test that would not be a distraction.

In 1976, Spelke *et al.* demonstrated the effect of practice. Participants were asked to read short stories for comprehension while taking dictation. Both tasks were poorly performed, but they received training and practice. Their reading speed and comprehension improved to the levels of performance they showed when not taking down dictation. However, they could recall very few of the dictated words. This suggested they might be attending to the task, but not the meaning of the words, another limitation to attention overcome with training.

Another difficulty experienced in divided attention is the similarity of the tasks. The dichotic listening tasks described above involve listening to two passages at the same time, but because they are in the same sensory modality and the passages are similar, attending to both is difficult. Much of the division we have discussed related to at least one task that is so familiar that it has become automatic.

AUTOMATIC

Automatic Processing

Complex tasks are initially difficult, but practice makes perfect (sometimes). At this point the performer no longer has to pay attention to what is going on. For example, think about learning to play the piano. A novice has to watch his or her fingers, a virtuoso does not. Striking the keys has become what is known as procedural; the player no longer needs to consciously remember the discrete steps used in the physical action, and it has become automatic.

procedural knowledge knowledge we have without necessarily being aware of what it is we know; implicit, tacit knowledge, as opposed to declarative knowledge, which is based entirely upon facts. We know what declaratively, we know how procedurally

So, fewer cognitive resources are needed to carry out underlying tasks and attention is not required. This seems to suggest that no task is too demanding once practised. The only limit to our processing ability is time to practise (or motivation) and hence achieve automatic processing.

In a similar way to physical activity reaching a state of *automaticity*, cognitive tasks can become automatic. One way of demonstrating this is the Stroop effect. This is a well established effect of reading *vs.* colour identification. The explanation is that reading can become such an automatic process that we have 'over-learnt' it to such an extent that not only can it be done automatically and efficiently, but it completely interferes with other tasks.

the Stroop effect when participants are presented with names of colours printed in an incongruous colour, e.g. red written with blue ink, etc., and have to name the ink colour rather than read the word, they find it very difficult to do. It appears that the tendency to read the names distracts from or interferes with attempts to name the colours (Stroop, 1935)

An automatic process occurs without any intention to do it. In the Stroop effect, the act of reading is a powerful process and takes over. It is also unconscious, and we do not have to think about it. It consumes few conscious processes, but does appear to override those that do on a simultaneous track. Automaticity then tells something about consciousness itself, an area of some debate in philosophy and all sciences of the mind, not just Cognitive Psychology. The next chapter will explore the idea of the mind and attention in terms of awareness and consciousness, areas of inference, and the neurology of attention.

Summary

The second point that information reaches, then, is where the mechanisms of attention and selection take over. Several theories produce models attempting to explain the way in which we identify and distinguish meaningful information. These models include bottleneck and capacity models, the former suggesting that stimuli are either filtered or tuned out before further processing, the latter postulating that limited resources are allocated for attending to stimuli. There are other things that mediate the process of attention, such as familiarity and practice. Some theorists would also suggest that attention can be the first point of cognitive awareness. In the next chapter we will examine the effect of awareness on information reaching our cognitive system.

Self-test Questions

1. Why are bottleneck theories of attention so called?
2. What would be the effect of attenuation?
3. Why are late selection models simpler than other bottleneck theories?
4. How does the resource allocation policy of capacity models work?
5. What does the Stroop effect demonstrate about automaticity?

Awareness, the Brain and Attention

Key terms

anoetic consciousness non-knowing
autonoetic consciousness self-knowing
brain asymmetry the different functions, and awareness of the left and right brain hemisphere
habituation the lack of response seen on repetitive presentation of a stimulus
noetic consciousness knowing
preconscious and unconscious memory different states of information, readily accessible, and unavailable respectively
reticular activating formation a brain structure associated with awareness

Key names

Posner • Sokolov • Tulving

Consciousness

Being aware of the environment appears to be required for cognition. This argument has been debated for many years. The questions are found in the writings of Greek philosophers, and we also find them discussed in the work of Wundt, James and Helmholtz. Consciousness is not a topic which is easily measured and analysed, but it is important for a discussion of attention because there appears to be a very close link. No discussion of Cognitive Psychology would be complete without a look, albeit briefly, at the effect awareness or consciousness has on mental processes.

Tulving (1985) is perhaps the first modern psychologist to explore and theorise in this area. He stated that there are three types of consciousness closely associated with three types of memory:

▶ anoetic – procedural memory
▶ noetic – semantic memory
▶ autonoetic – episodic memory.

See Chapters 6 and 7 for more discussion of memory.

43

Anoetic consciousness means 'non-knowing', in which we register environmental cues and respond to the current environment. It is temporally bound to the present.

Noetic means 'knowing', in which we are aware of things without having them in the current environment, a kind of symbolic consciousness.

Autonoetic means 'self-knowing', meaning that we remember personally experienced events.

This identification of distinct types of awareness means that the study of consciousness can be placed in the scientific sphere (Tulving, 1985). Previous to this cataloguing of consciousness, the study had remained in the less testable areas of philosophy and psychoanalysis. One area where it has been possible to produce scientific data is brain research in consciousness.

Consciousness and the Brain

In 1869, Broca identified brain asymmetry, the fact that different sides or hemispheres of the brain appear to have different functions. This led researchers to surmise that there may be two types of consciousness, an awareness of language in the left hemisphere, and spatial awareness in the right. This was proposed as a possible explanation of individual and cultural differences (Ornstein, 1977). This idea, as yet unclear, led to a lot of investigation and further classification of *levels* of consciousness. Each sensory modality has various levels of awareness. Sensations from each are reaching the cognitive system, but until attention is directed to them we remain relatively unaware of them. We can, it seems, direct our consciousness, but it is always operating on different levels. This has implications for how we might use attention, and also for what happens in memory. There are two roughly differentiated levels of access of information: that which is readily available, and that which is less so. The readily available, such as your own telephone number, is said to be in *preconscious* memory, and easily brought to conscious memory. The telephone number of that person you met at a party a month ago, however, is in *unconscious* memory, and sadly may never be recalled. Such ideas are still controversial due to the way that the psychoanalytical approach would maintain that information becomes unconscious.

However, the study of consciousness is still important for attention and memory. As attention has a limited capacity, perhaps one of the limitations is consciousness. Also the process of rehearsal, it is argued, is evidence of a consciousness at work (Shallice, 1972). Such arguments are not open to examination, but brain function is.

Neuropsychology of Attention

Modern developments in neuroscience have allowed us to examine the processes in the brain when it is working. It is still subject to a great deal of inferential input, however. Just because we 'see' electrical activity or changes in blood flow, it doesn't mean we are seeing the process at work. We can *infer* that when we ask a volunteer to remember something, and a portion of the brain changes, that this portion is dealing with memory.

> habituation with repeated presentation of a stimulus, there is a point at which the participant no longer reacts to it, and is said to have habituated to the stimulus. Activation, on the other hand, refers to the initial response

In attention, much research has been focused on the *reticular activating formation (RAF)*, a part of the midbrain which is connected to the cortex. It is often known as the arousal system. There are many other physiological reactions associated with attention, and those reactions appear to be connected to increase in blood flow in the brain. An influential model of the neurology of attention is that postulated by Sokolov (1960). Sokolov used EEG recordings to examine *habituation*. He noted that EEG arousal patterns disappeared with repeated presentation of stimuli. Cats were presented with auditory tones at set intervals, and exhibited habituation. However, if one tone was missed, the cats showed an *orienting* response, i.e. they turned their ears.

> orienting response the turning of the body, or parts of the body, with reference to the position of a stimulus in order to gain optimal exposure. Also the attentional response on the onset or absence of a stimulus, such as ear-pricking in some animals, or the widening of the pupils. In the latter case this is referred to as a reflex, not response, and it is one indication of emergence from a vegetative state. Lecturers see this all the time – when they stop speaking, students wake up

Sokolov's experiments led to a cortical model of attention. In this the brain is seen as an 'executive' which decides if information outside is at odds with that internal to the individual, and hence further arousal is needed. This does go some way to explaining findings from attention studies. Attenuation, for example, can be explained by habituation, cognitive energy being saved by tuning out stimuli which are constant or repetitive. This makes sense – we don't need to pay attention to tactile sensation from sitting on a chair, nor do we need to pay attention to automatic processes, so the level of consciousness is switched by the brain. Evidence for this kind of model does come from studying brain deficits.

Attention and the Brain

There appear to be specific areas of the brain associated with attention, as discovered by both the standard cognitive experimental techniques and the more direct brain scan methods (Mountcastle, 1978; Posner, 1988). All the evidence leads to the conclusion that there are separate areas of the brain dealing with attention, although interaction with other areas does take place. So it is neither the function of a single brain area, nor a collective function of the whole brain. There also appears to be specific activity in different anatomical areas supporting specific attentional function (Posner and

Petersen, 1990). Current knowledge relates to specific areas for the orienting response, detection, and maintenance of alertness. There are also indications of neurochemical influences on attention, with noradrenaline (norepinephrine) being particularly involved in alertness. Hyperactivity, now known to be a disorder due to attentional deficits, is associated with abnormalities of neurotransmission (Deutsch and Kinsbourne, 1990).

Summary

Consciousness is as yet ill defined, but we know it is concerned with awareness, and that it has effects on attention and memory. Given consciousness of a stimulus, we know whether individuals will habituate or orient to it. This leads us to be able to determine the activity of the brain and its part in attention.

Self-test Questions

1 What are the different forms of consciousness and how are they related to memory and awareness?
2 Why does habituation happen?
3 What evidence is there to suggest localisation of brain function with respect to attention?

PART 3

Information Storage

These chapters discuss how information is stored and organised. Memory systems (Chapter 6) process and transform information in storable forms, and place it in organised structures. It can be retrieved or lost at any stage of processing, so Chapter 7 looks at retrieval, and Chapter 8 looks at forgetting. Chapter 9 discusses how the retained information might be organised.

CHAPTER 6

The Structure of Memory

Key terms

articulatory or phonological loop a component of working memory concerned with holding verbal information

central executive a component of working memory which may identify processes that are needed

levels of processing a theory of how type and depth of processing affects retention

long term or permanent store a type of memory structure holding relatively large amounts of information, relatively permanently

multistore models a theory of how several components of memory are linked and work together

sensory store a type of memory structure that holds information from the immediate environment

serial position effect the effect seen when subjects recall word lists, with the first in the list (primacy effect) and the last in the list (recency effect) recalled better than the others

short term or transient store a type of memory structure holding information from the present, limited in capacity and fragile in nature

visuo-spatial sketch pad a component of working memory concerned with visual and spatial information

working memory a theory of how transient memory works

Key names

Anderson and Bower • Atkinson (and Shiffrin) (and Rundus) • Baddeley (and Hitch) • Bartlett • Bransford • Craik and Lockhart • Glanzer and Cunitz • Glenberg • Lashley • Loftus • Mandler • Miller • Paivio • Peterson and Peterson • Sperling

Memory is of concern to Cognitive Psychology because the storage and retrieval of information is fundamental to mental processes. There are several theories that claim to describe how memory works. What is clear from most is that there are different degrees of permanence of information in memory depending on what has happened to it. There is disagreement amongst theorists as to why this might be so. *Multistore theories* of memory contend that there are separate and distinct types of memory, called short term and long term memory. There may be a third, sensory store, which is the connection between attention and memory. An alternative theory is that there is only one store, but the different levels of processing that information undergoes make it permanent to greater or lesser degrees. Other approaches to memory suggest that the short term area is highly dynamic and active, and the links to the attentional system and to the long term store are a vigorous *working memory* system. This chapter will look at these three types or portions of memory, and how the theories have examined them and developed over the years. For convenience, and to be clear that no one theory is being considered over any other, the different types of memory will be discussed in terms of the nature of the information they hold rather than the nature of the store. So we will look at a sensory store (holding stimuli from the environment), a transient store (holding information which has short duration), and a permanent store.

Sensory Store

Information from the environment, in all sensory modalities, enters a sensory store. This idea overlaps with Broadbent's model of attention (see Chapter 4). All senses are involved, but the visual and auditory parts appear to have more salience. The visual store, often termed iconic, was examined by Sperling in 1960. Subjects were presented with a visual array of letters in a 3×4 matrix. They were shown this for 50 ms and could only recall a few, but knew that there were more. Sperling deduced that the visual image was available, but that it was transient in nature. Similarly the presence of the auditory (or echoic) store can be postulated by the 'what did you say?' phenomenon. Imagine you are reading and your companion asks you a question. Often you reply 'what did you say?', but then realise what the question was. It is almost as if you have 'played back' the last few moments of auditory experience. Due to this kind of event, it is generally thought that echoic storage is a little longer than iconic. Multistore theories, such as that developed by Atkinson and Shiffrin (1968), suggest that it is only when

Figure 6.1 *The multistore model*

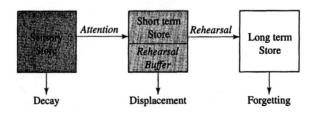

Decay   Displacement   Forgetting

attention is paid to information in the sensory store that it can go to the transient store. Figure 6.1 shows how the multistore model works.

Transient Store

Think about trying to remember a telephone number you have just been given. You need to use this number only once. What happens to it demonstrates several features of transient store.

1 Fragility. If you are interrupted on the way to the telephone with this new number, it will have 'disappeared', and you will have to go back to Directory Enquiries.
2 Limited capacity. It is difficult to remember much more than about eight digits. In 1956 Miller demonstrated that capacity is 7±2 chunks. As British telephone numbers are now 11 digits, perhaps there is a little problem here. What we tend to do is group items together.

There are several studies demonstrating transient store and its workings. Glanzer and Cunitz (1966) allowed subjects to perform free recall on a list of words. The words were presented, and immediately participants attempted to recall them in whatever order they wished. They found that there is good recall for the first few words (now called the primacy effect) and the last few (recency effect), but poorer recall for those in the middle. The longer the list, the more marked these effects become. An interference task immediately after the presentation of the list reduces recency, but not other items. They concluded the primacy effect was due to words entering a more permanent store, and therefore having a more permanent retention. The recency effect was due to these words being in short term, more temporary store, hence interruption stops their recall. The middle words had gone from transient store, pushed out by later items, but had not reached permanent store.

Another classic study on transient store was made in 1959 by Peterson and Peterson. Participants were given an item, followed by distractor tasks of different duration, until a cue was given for recall. The probability of recall decreased with the increase in the duration of the distractor. The conclusion was that the task had prevented participants from 'rehearsing' the item, and hence delayed processing long enough for it to disappear, and not reach permanent memory.

So transient store is of limited capacity and the information is held in a fragile form. It also appears that there is some organisation, unlike the sensory store. To return to this 7±2 business, these figures refer to 'chunks', not just single digits. The more associations between items, the more individual items can be represented. If numbers are presented as an unrelated list:

9 4 2 3 6 4 8 1 3 5

probable recall would be about 7. But if someone read them out

....ety-four, twenty-three, sixty-four, eighty-one, thirty-five

recall would probably be better. Consider

$$1 \quad 0 \quad 6 \quad 6 \quad 1 \quad 4 \quad 9 \quad 2 \quad 1 \quad 9 \quad 6 \quad 9$$

How much easier to remember

1066   1492   1969

The items have been chunked, and some encoding has taken place, so they are easier to reproduce in total.

The multistore model indicates that information is held in transient store via rehearsal and coding, i.e. some processing takes place in transient store in order to attach more information to it. The rehearsal buffer has a limited number of slots, each donated by the 'age' of the information held. Items coming in displace the newest, and the latest can only be retained if a slot is vacated by either the oldest going to permanent store or losing the next newest. The buffer also allows for different types of processing prior to long term retention. Rundus (1977) found that if subjects were allowed to rehearse words in a recall list task, they would rehearse those that were conventionally found to be recalled better in the primacy effect. In other words, if you allow subjects to make their own rehearsal strategy they would rehearse the first few words. If they are forced to give equal amounts of rehearsal to the full list, then the primacy effect is reduced (but not eliminated). However, Weist (1972) found that giving a list organised into semantic categories can also influence recall. Therefore it is not just the amount of rehearsal that is involved here, but something else. Craik and Lockhart (1972) proposed that there were two types of rehearsal involved: maintenance (repetition) and elaborative (a deeper analysis). The latter leads to better retention. This is known as the levels of processing theory. It suggests that the deeper the processing of information, the better it is retained. Deeper processing in this case means paying more

> paradigm a formalised approach to a problem or set of research investigations

attention to information, organising it and relating it to existing knowledge. The *paradigm* under which this model can be examined is one in which participants are asked not to memorise word lists, but to answer one of the following types of questions about them:

1 Whether the word was lower or upper case.
2 Whether the word rhymed with something else.
3 Whether the word described the participant.

The first is a physical processing, and led to the poorest recall performance. The second is an acoustic processing, and was better, but the best performance came from those words processed under the third category, semantic.

So the levels of processing theory would say that memory is influenced by internal factors, verbal and linguistic processing. There is a third, however: imagery. Paivio (1979) described these internal factors in a theory known as the dual-code theory, and suggested that verbal and non-verbal information is processed by two different but interconnected symbolic systems. Each system has auditory and visual aspects, but the *coding* is different. For example, we know that we have better memory for pictures than for words. Tunes are remembered before words (ask any singer!). Words that have better connections to images are recalled more easily. This is one of the ways in which it is claimed you can improve your memory, by improving your imagery.

So we have evidence that the transient store can pass information on to a long term store depending on the amount and type of rehearsal. This does not seem to reflect real life, however. Sometimes we do rehearse things in order to 'learn' them, but it is not likely that everything reaches permanent memory in this way. An alternative proposition was outlined in 1974 by Baddeley and Hitch. Transient memory is a dynamic and organised system, rather than the passive area merely performing rehearsal implied by other theories. Memory is a system that provides temporary storage and manipulation of the information necessary for complex cognitive tasks. Baddeley and Hitch suggested this area should be called *working memory*, with several components to it:

1 Central executive
2 Articulatory loop
3 Visuo-spatial sketch pad
4 Primary acoustic store.

The central executive is actually describing attention, as it is operating in all modalities, and determines whether or not the other systems are to be used. There has been little research on the central executive, and its existence is in dispute. Later theories of working memory suggest that the way in which it is supposed to work simply shows interactions between the other components. It is true that something must be identifying what processes, rehearsal, imagery, retrieval, etc. need to be carried out, and it might be something like the central executive. Norman and Shallice (1980) suggested that the central executive is a 'supervisory attentional system' regulating lower level automatic processes.

The articulatory loop is also sometimes called the phonological loop. It is the facility you are using when you repeat things to yourself in order to remember them. This is often referred to as the 'inner voice' or subvocalising when learning. The phonological processes can be subject to the following problems, which suggest that it is really there.

► Suppression – by interfering with rehearsal.

Figure 6.2 *Loop length illustration*

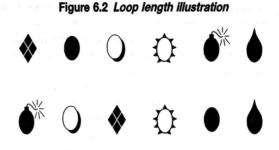

▶ Confusion – similar items can become replacements for each other, and one is lost. For example, we often confuse letters that are the same, or similar telephone numbers.

▶ Loop length – the shorter the set of things to be remembered, the better is subsequent recall. Imagine trying to recall a sequence of items of different colours such as that shown in Figure 6.2. If you remember the first sequence as two black, two white, two black, then that is a short description and it will be remembered better. The second one, when described as *first, third, fifth and sixth black,* makes for too long a description.

▶ Word length – when many things must be remembered, then the shorter the words involved, the better.

It appears that spoken words enter the articulatory loop, and produce memory traces. Written words are converted into phonological code, then enter the loop. These memory traces fade very quickly, but can be refreshed by sub-vocalising or rehearsal.

The visuo-spatial sketch pad deals with, as its name suggests, the visual and spatial information, and the requisite processing. This includes using imaged mnemonics, spatial reasoning, planning and orientation.

The primary acoustic store is often referred to as the 'inner ear'. This appears to be the component that works on the 'what did you say?' phenomenon discussed above.

Working memory is an interesting theory, and work is still progressing on it. It does seem to be a reasonable explanation for many phenomena associated with transient memory: see Baddeley (1992).

Permanent Store

If sensory store is concerned with the immediate, and transient store is concerned with the psychological present, then we can define permanent store as concerned with the psychological past. As the name suggests, it is a more 'permanent' storage place. The multistore models would suggest that all knowledge is kept in one large, long term store, but this seems a little naive. No one would organise their warehouse so that everything was simply placed all together in one heap, so why would our memories be like that? Alternative theorists would say that there are several different types of permanent memory. The distinctions are between either episodic and semantic memory or declarative and procedural memory.

Episodic memory contains information which is autobiographical in content, whereas semantic memory is an organised repository of world knowledge. This differentiation between two types of memory was first made by Tulving in 1972. Tulving observed that there is memory for personally experienced events and memory for general world knowledge. The alternative idea is of declarative and procedural memory, declarative being that information to which we have conscious access, and is concerned with knowing what, whereas procedural is knowing how, and includes skill and expertise.

Episodic and Semantic Memory

Tulving's work was particularly concerned with *encoding*, and developed the *encoding specificity principle* in terms of memory. This means that only information that has been stored can be retrieved, and how it was stored influences how it is retrieved. Tulving demonstrated that episodic and semantic memory are different systems, by examining encoding specificity. In 1973 Tulving and Thomson asked participants to learn 24 pairs of words, one in upper and one in lower case, which were only weakly associated. One word was the weak cue and the other the target. The participants were then shown 12 words which were strongly associated with some of the original 24 targets. So for example the associations might be:

> encoding the transformation of items from one form to another. So on hearing a sentence the listener codes it as acoustic events, which are then encoded as words

Weak cue	Target	Strong cue
light	WINDOW	*glass*

Recall was quite poor, about two words.

Another 12 strong cues were given for the other 12 of the original 24 targets. The participants had to think of words that were associated with the 12 strong cues, and if a word appeared in the capitalised words, they had to write it down. Recall went up to about three or four.

Participants were then asked to free associate all of the 24 strong cues and recall rose to about 18 of the 24 targets, but only recognised about four as coming from the original list.

Finally, those still speaking to the experimenters were given the weak cues again, and asked to recall the targets, and they recalled about 15. So, participants were able to generate words, but not necessarily able to recognise them. People were generating words in response to strong cues that had been associated with the weak cues, but not recognising them. Tulving and Thomson were seeing *recognition failure of recallable events*. This shows that an ability to remember depends on encoding, and that the weak cues were better retrieval cues than the strong because the latter were not part of the *episodic* memories. They are part of the semantic memories, but the recognition failure is using episodic (experiential) events, not semantic ones. This does show evidence for the two types of memory. There is also evidence that the two types of memory develop differently and that ageing affects them differently, perhaps accounting for the often surprising recall abilities of the elderly.

Declarative and Procedural Memory

Even if episodic and semantic memory are different structures, there are similarities. They involve declarative knowledge. As stated above, declarative knowledge is that using facts, things that we 'know what'. However, we also 'know how' to do things, like type a letter or essay. The distinction between these two types of memory and their relationship with episodic and semantic memory will be explored in the next chapter.

Implicit and Explicit Memory

Finally a word about testing memory, and what that shows about the nature of permanent store. Many laboratory tests of memory involve free recall, cued recall and recognition measurement. These involve specific experience recalled under direct instruction, and are therefore explicit. Studies using patients with some form of amnesia (see the next chapter) show that they are markedly poorer than non-amnesiacs. When other forms of measurement are used, however, and more implicit memory is examined, these differences disappear. Such tests might be word completion (see Graf *et al.*, 1984) which accesses a more subtle area of memory. The distinction between them is still unclear, however.

The Site of Memory

It would be easy to imagine that the above models describe a tangible physical structure somewhere in the brain. It would have made it so much easier to study if this were the case. There is some evidence, however, to suggest that memory does have a physical, biological basis.

The crudest indications that there is a neural basis for memory come from Lashley's (1929) experiments on learning in rats. Lashley performed progressive cortex and subcortical extirpation (he cut out bigger and bigger parts of the rats' brains from the outer layer known as the cortex and structures lying below it). After a certain amount of damage, the rats could no longer perform as well in maze learning and visual discrimination tasks (and he was surprised?). From these studies Lashley developed the theory of mass action, and the principle of equipotentiality. These suggest that cognitive functions are spread around the brain.

> mass action cognitive function is not dependent on specific neuronal areas, but distributed throughout the brain
> equipotentiality if one part of the brain is damaged, no one specific function is affected, as other portions of the brain are performing them. This is true up to a maximum amount of damage, so all areas of the brain have equal potential to carry out any function.

This might not be the full story, however. In 1959, Penfield found that electrical stimulation of highly specific areas of the cortex in conscious patients could make particular muscles twitch, and, in a small proportion of individuals, lead to recall of specific memories. Data from psychophysiological studies suggest that neuro-electrical characteristics of brain structures change during learning or recall. Nowadays we can examine brain scans showing blood flow and electrical activity. These show that, for example, different parts of the brain are more active when episodic memory is being used than when someone is using semantic processing (Tulving, 1989). Such studies do lead to the conclusion that, even given mass action and equipotentiality, the memory represented by abstract psychological models is to be found in the frontal lobe and the hippocampus and amygdala, but that it might be certain combinations of sets of neurones that are being used (Rosenweig, 1996).

It was at one time supposed that information might be stored as electrical activity in the brain, a feasible suggestion. Electrical activity is continuous and can reverberate (pass around neural circuits). But if this accounts for permanent memory, any disruption such as epilepsy or electroconvulsive interventions (there is a reluctance to call this latter treatment or therapy) should affect not only immediate memory, but the permanent too. This does not appear to be the case; people experiencing epilepsy do not have generalised memory loss, but some specific problems with transient memory. Those having ECT inflicted on them do have disruption to transient memory, but permanent memory impairment might be more associated with physical damage. Whoever said this was safe and effective should reconsider. We will look more closely at the effects of illness and treatments in the next chapter.

It is clear that a large proportion of memory depends on permanent changes in neuronal structure, relatively small and allowing high detail. Plausibly these changes occur at synaptic junctions. An alternative hypothesis is that these changes are in the form of protein structure modifications.

It is beyond the scope of this book to examine all this biological evidence, but there is evidence that memory has a physical basis. Such evidence has implications for the study of memory, and the treatment of amnesia. It also adds to the confusion about the structure of memory.

Evidence for Models of Memory

Much of the biological evidence shows that different areas of the brain are activated during different tasks. Deficits in performance on tasks thought to be accessing spatial working memory have been shown after right temporal lobectomy. Feigenbaum *et al.* (1996) and Mecklinger and Muller (1996) suggest that different components of working memory have functionally and anatomically distinct brain structures associated with them. The central executive is thought to be accessed by dual-task performance. In comparison with single-task performance, the central executive is functioning due to the need to identify processes and allocate functional capacity. Magnetic resonance imaging monitored during dual-task performance showed prefrontal cortex activation (D'Esposito *et al.*, 1995). On the other hand, distinctions between short term and long term memory accessing tasks showed different brain structures being used. Guillem *et al.* (1996) used electrical probes to show posterior temporal cortex activation in short term memory, and limbic system use in long term, with the hippocampus implicated in maintaining memory traces. The levels of processing approach also has its biological support, in that the paradigm does affect the performance on recognition and explicit memory. This is different for 'normal' participants, and those who are amnesiac due to brain damage (Hamann and Squire, 1996).

What this really shows is that there are different areas in use depending on what you are doing with your memory. Rather than giving support for any one model, these studies appear to show that there are different functions in memory rather than different pieces of memory. Perhaps we should examine function rather than form and look at how memory works, and can be improved, rather than the shape or site of it.

Summary

We can see that there are definite areas of memory that perform differently. Evidence for a sensory store is good, but it may be a more active area than originally thought. There are also strong indications that a fragile, limited capacity area of memory acts on information to organise it and send it to a permanent storage area. This latter is highly organised and may comprise several parts. Various theories have attempted to build models to explain how these areas interact and work, and also where they are. What we need to look at now is not just how memory is constructed, but how it works, and how material is organised. The next chapters will discuss the processing of information in memory, how it is retained, how it is retrieved and why retrieval might fail.

Self-test Questions

1 What are the major distinctions between sensory store, transient store, and permanent store?
2 How can we demonstrate the serial position effect?
3 How would the levels of processing theory explain the fact that material can fail to reach long term store?
4 What different types of information are handled by the phonological loop and the visuo-spatial sketch pad?
5 In what ways can permanent memory be categorised?
6 Summarise the evidence that memory might have physical structure.

CHAPTER 7

Retention and Retrieval

Key terms

clustering a form of organisation in permanent store
information transfer the procedure by which information passes from transient to permanent store
memory codes evidence suggests that information is coded for organisation in transient store, codes being investigated including auditory, visual and semantic
recall a retrieval process of reconstruction
recognition a retrieval process of comparison
release from proactive inhibition a phenomenon in which it is more difficult to recall later items when earlier items have already been learnt
schemata, frames and scripts forms of organisation in permanent store
Sternberg paradigm an experimental procedure on which participants compare a probe with a memory set

Key names

Bartlett • Collins and Quillian • Conrad • Johnston • Mandler • Miller • Peterson and Peterson • Posner • Sternberg • Wickens

The last chapter examined how information gets into memory, and the evidence that it forms physical traces. There is some disagreement about whether there is a distinction between short term (or transient) and long term (or permanent) store or memory, and what form these structures might take. Here, however, we will use these terms for convenience, as we need to look at how information is stored and organised. It is clear that some material is held for only a short time, whereas some receives a more 'permanent' storage. Also, what happens to material in the short term appears to influence the probability of retention due to the structure it acquires. The organisation it has appears to influence retrieval. So there are two questions for the organisation of memory, short term and long term.

Organisation in Transient Store

The last chapter established that short term store, of whatever nature, is limited in capacity, fragile in nature, and short in duration, and that there are solid pieces of evidence to indicate the existence of this store. Its format could be either the separate store indicated by multistore models, a dynamic part of memory as in working memory, or an encoding facility indicated in the levels of processing theory. What is clear is that the functioning of this area is facilitated by several things: the ability to rehearse material will extend the cognitive life of information, and chunking of material will enlarge the capacity for items. Peterson and Peterson (1959, see Chapter 6) established that preventing people from rehearsing information makes the information susceptible to loss. Miller (1956) established that the capacity of a short term store was an immutable 7±2 items. However, this figure is not quite what it seems. As discussed in Chapter 6, chunking information together in some form of categorisation means that each of those 7±2 items can be very complex. Miller suggested that each item was occupying a slot in the short term storage area because they were *coded* in some way. Single items become coded as groups of linked items. This coding, though, needs some form of activation, and this must come from a long term representation. For example, you would not be able to chunk and retain the items from Chapter 6 unless you already knew the date of the Battle of Hastings, when Columbus landed in America, and the year Apollo 11 landed on the moon. So what kind of codes are used?

Auditory Coding

Think about remembering that telephone number again. What do you do? You probably repeat it to yourself until you get the chance to dial it (unless you have the opportunity to write it down). Repeating it in this way means you are making an auditory representation of the number in transient store. This intuitive knowledge about how transient store works has been tested in the laboratory. Conrad (1963) looked at recall errors when letters were presented visually or spoken. Some letters were those that sounded alike, and participants made errors on the basis of the similar sounds, even when they were presented visually. Conrad concluded from this, and other similar studies, that transient store was acoustic in nature. This is not necessarily the full story, however.

Visual Coding

Posner's work suggests that there may also be a form of visual coding in transient store. If subjects are shown two letters in the form Aa, AA, AB or Ab, then asked to press a button to indicate whether they are the same letter irrespective of case, the reaction time is longer for Aa than AA. The conclusion here is that identical letters are judged on the basis of visual characteristics, but letters with the same sound, although different physical appearance, are compared on their verbal characteristics. The verbal checking takes longer, suggesting that visual coding happens before acoustic (Posner *et al.*, 1969).

Semantic Coding

If auditory and visual codes are used in transient store, then might there not be a place for attaching meaning to items too? Several pieces of evidence suggest that this is so. Wickens and colleagues in 1963 looked at proactive inhibition (PI) which simply means that it is more difficult to recall later items when earlier items have already been learnt. They used the idea that when learning a series of related words, testing after each set of, for example, three words, recall is best after the first set, then gets progressively poorer with each new set. Switching to a different series means the new series will be recalled better than the last set of the original series. Wickens called this 'release from PI'. What Wickens did was show participants a set of words, then make them do a distractor task, then recall. Doing this for four successive trials, the last trial was different. The control group would learn another set related to the first three sets, but the experimental group would get a different category: see Figure 7.1.

The experimental group performed far better in trial 4 than the control group. It appears that some form of semantic organisation is being used; the control group is continuing to use the 'slot' for dogs, and this is being used up, whereas the experimental group have a new fresh slot available. This inference has some criticisms. Firstly, there has to be a connection with the stored concepts for the coding to take place. However, there has never been any suggestion that the temporary and permanent storage systems do not have some kind of reciprocal relationship. Secondly, the experiment described above does take time, and this might be beyond the duration of transient store, and may be accessing long term memory anyway. There is

Figure 7.1 *Proactive inhibition experiment*

All subjects								
Trial 1			Trial 2			Trial 3		
Poodle Collie Greyhound	Distractor	Recall	Whippet Alsatian Sheepdog	Distractor	Recall	Terrier Dachshund Beagle	Distractor	Recall

Trial 4					
Experimental Group			Control Group		
Mother Father Baby	Distractor	Recall	Setter Rottweiler Labrador	Distractor	Recall

other evidence for semantic coding in transient store, though. If participants are given four words, then asked to identify whether three other words are in the original set, they will identify correctly some as being there or not, but semantically related words do cause 'false alarms'. For example, the following four words are presented:

SEAT
BENCH
SOFA
SETTEE

Then the next set:

CHAIR
PEW
BENCH

Participants correctly identify PEW as being new, and BENCH as being in the original set, but CHAIR can become confused. Its semantic relationship with the original set leads to misidentification. This will take place in a very short space of time, and is well within the limits of transient store. This kind of experiment was carried out by Sternberg (1966), and does show how information is accessed in and retrieved from transient store.

Retrieval from Transient Store

Sternberg (1966, 1969) was very influential in establishing that material in transient store may need some form of retrieval machanism, as previously it was thought that all material was available *whilst it was still there* and had not been lost. We have already said that the transient store, or temporary memory, is concerned with the psychological present (James, 1890), and it seemed that everything that was in the store could be accessed. However items are organised, some with a different coding system from others, then perhaps some information is better retrieved, and the others are not lost, just more difficult to access. As transient store is a temporary store, this would seem to be dependent on the speed of access, and the Sternberg paradigm examines this very neatly.

The Sternberg Paradigm

Between one and six items (the 'memory set') are presented to the participants. Shortly afterwards a 'probe' is presented, and the participants have to decide if the probe matches one of the memory set. Few errors are made; what is interesting is the speed of response in relation to the size of the memory set. Sternberg found that the results are consistent with participants comparing the probe against each of the items in the set at about 25–30 per second. They are apparently performing a serial (one-by-one) exhaustive (eliminating until found) search. If this is what they are doing, then positive matches should terminate, and therefore be quicker than negative ones where no match is to be found. This is so, but not to a significant degree, and anyway, what if you increase the size of the memory set? If you add to the memory set, then the time should increase, but at twice the rate for the negative responses (or thereabouts, depending on where positive matches are placed). This does not happen, so there is something else going on. Sternberg proposed a total of four stages including this serial comparison one. Before this takes place, there is the time taken to process the probe itself, and recognise what it is, then the serial comparison, then a decision time (whether to say 'yes' or 'no'), then organising the response. The comparison time is such a small part of all this, that the differences between positive matching and negative responses are minimal. There are a few problems with this, however. People just can't leave well alone, and noticed that there is a recency effect, in which the reaction time is quicker if the probe matches one of the last few of the set. If the participants are carrying out an exhaustive search, it should not matter where the match is sited. The possibility here is that, the stronger or more familiar the probe is, the quicker the comparison is performed. Also if the memory set is larger, then the overall familiarity of the set declines, and the more recent items have greater strength. Atkinson and Juola (1974) proposed that both of these possibilities might be true, and that very low familiarity could account for a quick search. This model accounts neatly for both the Sternberg findings and the slight inconsistencies.

So retrieval from transient store does appear to involve a search, but is also linked to long term memory, and the probability of retrieving information to use. What is also of interest is how information gets from transient store to its long term equivalent.

Information Transfer

Essentially, the process we determined that was acting on information was rehearsal. Rehearsal is an attempt to encode information, to transform it into acceptable, useful forms. The codes that the encoding process attaches to material can be acoustic, visual or semantic. If information cannot be encoded, then the likelihood is that it cannot be stored in a meaningful form. It would seem that it is the nature of rehearsal that determines the probability of passing information to long term, and it subsequent durability. Using the classic levels of processing set-up described in Chapter 6, Bellazza (1993) showed not only the distinction between the three levels, but a difference within semantic coding too. If participants fill in gaps in simple and complex sentences, they later recall more words from the complex sentences. So there appears to be not only rehearsal involved, but also the cognitive structures being accessed.

Bransford *et al.* (1977) also established that there is a transfer-appropriate type of processing, in that recall is better when cues are appropriate to the type of processing that went on during rehearsal.

So we know that transient store is limited, but organised, whatever form it takes, and whatever we call it. We know that a great deal of processing does on in it and that this facilitates both the use and transfer of information to permanent store. What we need to know now is what happens to information in the long term area. Firstly, we will examine theories and research looking at how information is retrieved from long term, and secondly at how this throws light on how it might be organised.

Retrieval from Long Term Store (Permanent Store)

There are two activities carried out when retrieving information from a more permanent store – recognition and recall.

Recognition

An example of recognition is seeing a face of an actor whilst watching *Casablanca* and trying to retrieve the name, whereas recall is trying to remember who starred in *Casablanca*. Or perhaps something a little closer to home: recognition is taking a multiple-choice exam, where the correct answer is there in front of you in a choice of four or five, and recall is trying to work out what on earth the examiner means by this particular essay title.

> recognition comparison of incoming information with items already encoded and stored
> recall the production of cues, which are not present in the environment, to aid the retrieval of information

Consider that multi-choice state. Seeing an answer may bring about feelings of familiarity, or definitely not, or ambiguity – the last would initiate a slower search of memory. This introspective evidence has suggested that retrieval is therefore a two-stage process:

▶ assessment of familiarity
▶ self-directed searches.

The assessment of familiarity is determined by an item's *perceptual fluency* (Johnson *et al.*, 1985). If you can identify a tune even though you are distracted by speech (that cocktail party again) then the tune has perceptual fluency. So we use fluency to judge whether something has been recognised. When perceptual fluency is low, the second process is used to check whether something has been encoded at some stage. Johnston *et al.* suggested the two processes work together. They investigated this theory by a set of experiments. Participants read a list of uncommon words presented on a computer screen, then were told there would be a test. They had to identify obscured words (obscured by randomly positioned dots, which were gradually removed) as quickly as possible by reading them aloud, then decide if it was in the original list or not. The shorter response time indicated greater perceptual fluency. Therefore, words from the list, which should have greater perceptual fluency, should have quicker response times, and accuracy of identification should be better. If a new word is judged to be on the list when it was not (a false alarm), then this also should be quicker. If the participant is using familiarity judgements, the assessment of familiarity should come into play when making false alarms. This proved to be the case: correct judgements *and* false alarms were quicker than for rejections, suggesting perceptual fluency was being used for judging the words. But there were inconsistencies. When the participants got it completely wrong, and they judged an old word new, this should have been slower than false alarms. It was not, so something other than perceptual fluency was being used. The hypothesis was that this is a search procedure of some kind. Johnston's second experiments included pronounceable non-words, to exclude the possibility of memory for coding and reduce the usefulness of a search. This forced participants to use familiarity, rather than memory. The time for false alarms was reduced to below that of the misses. So recognition does appear to involve two processes working together.

Encoding specificity (see Chapter 6) follows the transfer-appropriate idea of Bransford; the cue must match the context in which the item was encoded. This would apply equally well in terms of both recognition and recall, however.

Recall

Whilst it appears that recognition is a very powerful form of retrieval, studies of recall show that participants can recall things they do not recognise. There appear to be two types of recall: the recall of information that is always available, such as your address, and recall of information that is a selection amongst several plausible alternatives, such as a friend's telephone number. Studies of recall have tended to be dominated by verbal material, as visual material is poorly recalled, except in cases of *eidetic* memory.

> eidetic memory sometimes called photographic memory, in which a memory image can possess the accuracy and detail of a photograph. This can work for auditory memory too

Two methods of study have been employed to examine recall: free recall and cued recall. Free recall is assumed to access retrieval procedures for information that is easily accessible, and which does not require *intrinsic* information (that provided specifically to aid in retrieval). Cued recall is thought to work in one of two days. Given encoding specificity, cued recall will be successful when the cue matches the original stored information. There is another possibility in that the cue need not directly match. This is the generate–recognise hypothesis (Bahrick, 1970). Information related to the cue is generated in memory, and it is assessed as to whether it matches the target. These two mechanisms appear separate and exclusive, although evidence can be provided to show that recall can be both direct access and indirect (see Jones, 1987).

There are other factors which seem to influence recall. A memory made during an emotional experience can be recalled with great accuracy. A well-known example of this is that every adult American can (apparently) remember exactly where they were when they heard that J.F. Kennedy had been shot. This is known as a *flashbulb memory*, and emotional content and uniqueness are factors in recalling the event (Sadowski and Quast, 1990).

> free recall an experimental set-up in which participants are shown a word list and subsequently attempt to recall words, usually in any order
> cued recall an experimental set-up in which participants are provided with cues at recall. Cues are information related in some way to the information to be recalled, e.g. a list of word pairs, with one member of the pair being used as a cue for the recall of the other word

Recall and recognition, then, are seen to involve different processes. Cues are important in both, but the nature of the cue is different. Organisation of material affects recall performance more than recognition, probably because recall requires more complex processes. We need to look at organisation of information in permanent store in more detail.

Organisation in Long Term Store

All of the above does suggest that memory is highly organised, and that the better organisation is, the better retrieval will be. Organisation can be demonstrated very easily. If participants are given sets of words in categories, but presented randomly, then asked to free recall, they will tend to recall them not randomly but in the categories. This is known as categorical clustering.

Clustering

We have already determined that information in transient store is chunked into related items. According to a clustering model, information is held in permanent stores in clusters. Mandler (1967) presented participants with random lists of words, and asked them to sort them into categories. Some were asked to use two, some three, up to seven categories. Then they were asked to recall them. Those that used higher numbers of categories recalled more. So when people impose a structure on information, recall is better.

Semantic Memory

The idea that some sort of organisation can be used to store information led to theories of semantic memory. Early theories proposed a hierarchical network, with concepts stored as nodes, and properties or features associated

Figure 7.2 *Collins and Quillian's hierarchical model of semantic memory*

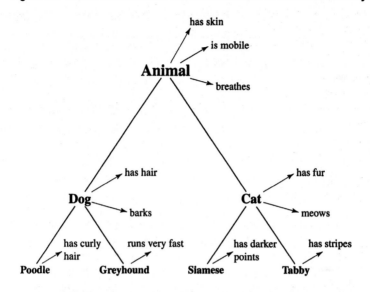

with each node (Collins and Quillian, 1969). Thus the organisation of the categories dog and cat, as sub-categories of animal, would be represented as shown in Figure 7.2. The model also incorporates two new ideas that Collins and Quillian proposed: intersecting searches, and inheritance hierarchies. An intersecting search is a method for finding connection between two concepts. Activation starts at the nodes, then spreads to those directly connected to them, then outwards. When the activation meets, the path is tested to see if it verifies a supposed relation. Inheritance hierarchy means that nodes will inherit properties from those above them in the net.

The further up the hierarchy information is stored, the more generalised it is, with specific information only needing to be stored with examples of the category. This was tested by asking participants to decide whether statements were true or false. So a decision on 'a tabby has stripes' should be very quick because this information is stored at the same level of the hierarchy, but sentences like 'a tabby barks' or 'a poodle has skin' should be longer, as the hierarchy has to navigate along several lines before making a decision. This makes a great deal of sense, particularly when we examine making inferences. For example, we can infer that HM Queen Elizabeth has elbows, even though that information is not necessarily part of the normal repertoire of our everyday lives.

Unfortunately there are several problems with the semantic network theory, and we will examine it in more detail in Chapter 9. Suffice to say that organisation into categories and sub-categories is quite a pleasing idea, and is certainly not counter-intuitive.

Schemata

Words and single ideas are not the only pieces of information that are stored in memory. Bartlett (1932) proposed that much larger chunks of material, called *schemata*, were also stored. He proposed that sequences of events will lead to the construction of a mental representation. His well-known study concerns asking participants to remember a story called 'The War of the Ghosts'. This story, from North American Indian culture, was unfamiliar to the participants, who were English, and Bartlett found that they tended to eliminate the peculiarities of the story, making it closer to their own culture. The distortions, said Bartlett, were due to the stored schemata of the participants, and they were rationalising. For example, in the story, a man died after 'something black came out of his mouth'; the participants recalled this as 'foaming at the mouth'. There was also flattening (not remembering unfamiliar ideas) and sharpening (elaborating). Criticisms of the study include the fact that some errors disappear when participants are told to avoid inaccuracies. But the study has been replicated many times with the same findings. Retrieval appears to be a process of reconstruction using stored patterns. Later theorists use the terms *frames* or *scripts* to describe these stored structures.

> **schema, schemata (pl.)** a coherent collection of material concerning an event, objects, etc

Summary

Several models of memory have been proposed, but all agree that some information is transient in nature with respect to our cognitive system, and some receives a more permanent encoding and storage. All the evidence also shows that there is some organisation taking place, or memory cannot be used effectively. There is strong evidence that organising material, even as late as retrieval time, improves memory, at least for text (Mann and Brenner, 1996). What remains is to examine why memory might not work as we might wish. The next chapter will look at a phenomenon that has perplexed psychologists for centuries: forgetting.

Self-test Questions

1　Why might transient store codes not be wholly auditory in nature?
2　What is the Sternberg paradigm?
3　What might limit the transfer of information from transient to permanent store?
4　What are the differences between the processes occurring in recognition and recall?
5　What are the differences between clustering and semantic networks?

CHAPTER 8

Erm ... Forgetting

Key terms

anterograde amnesia inability to encode new information
cognitive interview interviews with eye-witnesses designed to raise the integrity and amount of information gained
cue-dependent forgetting loss of retrieval cues leads to loss of information
decay a theory of forgetting in which memory traces decay
dissociative amnesia a psychogenic form of amnesia associated with trauma
dissociative fugue a psychogenic state involving almost total memory loss, and hence identity loss; often temporary
dissociative identity disorder multiple personality disorders associated with high levels of repression due to sustained trauma or abuse. Or faking
interference a theory of forgetting in which information competes for space
organic states brain dysfunction associated with amnesia, including head injury, strokes, alcoholism and degenerative diseases of the brain
proactive inhibition old material interfering with new
psychogenic states psychiatric problems associated with amnesia
repression motivated forgetting due to memory being too painful for recall
retroactive inhibition new material interfering with old
retrograde amnesia inability to recall past events
state-dependent forgetting loss of information due to the retrieval state being different from the cueing state
trace-dependent forgetting loss of memory trace leads to forgetting
Wernicke's encephalopathy degeneration in the brain leading to memory disorders. Associated with thiamine deficiency, often linked to alcoholism, when it is known as Korsakoff's syndrome, although this can have other causes than alcohol abuse

Key names

Ebbinghaus • Eich • Fisher and Geiselman • Freud • Godden and Baddeley • Jenkins and Dallenbach • Kopelmann • Korsakoff • Lindsay and Johnson • Loftus • Overton • Schachter • Tulving • Wernicke • Wilson • Whitten and Leonard

The question of why we forget has perplexed theorists. In terms of formal psychological theories, finding the answer is hampered by not having a universally accepted theory of memory. However, for every model of memory, there is an accompanying model of forgetting. Forgetting can mean many things, but we all have some idea of what it means to us. In lay terms, forgetting is often associated with the dramatic. Cases of amnesia often become the subject of thrillers. In fact amnesia is less frequent than might be supposed, and studying it can tell us a great deal about memory. In this chapter we will look at 'everyday' forgetting that affects us all, and then amnesia.

Theories of Forgetting

Recall of items does not remove them from memory, indeed the more often an item is remembered, the more fixed it seems to become. But if it is never recalled and left in store indefinitely, does it become erased, or links to it erased? It has been shown that outside interference during the learning process lowers recall ability and prevents, for example, the recency effect from appearing, but this is loss from transient store. Forgetting in permanent store has traditionally been attributed to one of two processes – unlearning (trace decay) and competition (interference). Decay theories interpret forgetting as the result of spontaneous fading, or weakening with time, of a neural memory trace. Interference theories, on the other hand, argue that forgetting is caused by subsequent events which make the trace less accessible.

Interference

Consider the paired associate paradigm. Competition occurs between responses when two or more responses have been associated with one stimulus prompt. The retrieval of one blocks or interferes with the retrieval of the other. Suppose a participant has just learnt an A-B, A-C sequence. Interference theory allows for the weakening of an associative link between the originally learnt pair, when the second pair is learnt. This is very much like the idea of extinction of a conditioned response. If the participants are given two word pair lists and asked to learn both, but retrieve C given A, what happens when they retrieve B? It is not rewarded or reinforced, as it is an error. But the participants are likely to recall B every time A-C is repeated, so the non-reward of B means the link is progressively inhibited. You also have aggrieved participants who go home vowing never to take part in a psychology experiment again!

There also appear to be two types of interference demonstrated: new material can interfere with old (retroactive inhibition, RI) or old material interferes with new learning (proactive inhibition, PI, or you can't teach an old dog new tricks). Both are shown quite clearly in the paired associate experiments.

Behavioural theories would simply say that the stimulus–response link has been weakened, and would not seek to explain the different types of interference. Cognitive Psychology looks for a little more complexity and inference than that, and does not ignore evidence. We also note that the nice neat demonstration of interference in the laboratory does not always occur in real life. Tulving's distinction between episodic and semantic memory might help here. The paired associate learning would appear to conform to the episodic memory idea, but implies that stronger links are made between items due to semantic memory. Hence it depends on the amount and type of encoding whether or not items interfere with each other. Neatly explained, but why does material still 'disappear' from memory? Let us turn to decay theories for an explanation.

Decay

Decay theory would say that material that remains unused for a long period actually decays. If we grant that memory leads to neural traces, we know that the central nervous system decays with age, so perhaps this accounts for the loss of material in memory? An attractive hypothesis, and one which is certainly not counter-intuitive, but it does not take into account events occurring between learning and recall. In 1924, Jenkins and Dallenbach reported greater loss of memorised material in participants who went about their normal activities (which can be supposed to have an interfering effect) than in those who slept between learning and recall. Ebbinghaus (1885), serving as his own subject, quantified the amount of forgetting, demonstrating that the rate of forgetting started as rapid, then slowed down.

An alternative to decay theory is obliteration, in that memory traces need time to become established, and the quicker some event occurs after learning, the quicker a memory can be destroyed. This evidence comes from work with fish and electric shocks, however, and it is unclear exactly what comparison between fish and humans can be drawn.

So, we are led to a position, as yet undefined, combining the two theories. We need to look more closely at this. Tulving (1974) distinguished between two types of forgetting. Trace-dependent forgetting simply means that the memory trace has decayed, and therefore is lost. This is a bit difficult to examine, even if it seems to make sense. Cue-dependent forgetting, on the other hand, means that the information is still stored, but is inaccessible because the retrieval cue has been lost.

Cue-dependent Forgetting

This theoretical aspect of forgetting is closely associated with encoding specificity (see Chapter 6). If our knowledge of something has been encoded in a particular way, then trying to retrieve it under a different set of circumstances will fail. So if your lecturer does not acknowledge you when you see her shopping in the supermarket, it is not rudeness, she simply is used to seeing you in the lecture hall, not the grocery section. The information is coded in highly specific extrinsic context.

> **context** how contextual factors determine memory coding. Extrinsic context is incidental background to the information, such as the fact that students are most often seen in the lecture hall or seminar room. Intrinsic context is the specifics to the information, such as the fact that an individual student may have red hair

Changes in intrinsic information do reduce the ability to recall, but extrinsic context changes are very interesting. Godden and Baddeley (1975) showed that when participants learnt information underwater, the subsequent recall was better if they remained submerged (and they got volunteers for this?). The fact that recall is better in the environment where the encoding took place has implications for a real-life situation.

Eye-witness Testimony

The widespread dependence of legal evidence on eye-witness testimony belies its undeniable problems. Eye-witness testimony (we will use this term to cover all sorts of evidence from observers of a crime, not just the visual information) is often faulty due to problems of perception or memory. How often have you seen some dramatisation of a court scene where the witness is shown to be wrong in their statement by some 'clever' lawyer, who points out they could not possibly have seen or heard what they are swearing to have witnessed? According to several researchers (see Loftus, 1975, 1979; Lindsay and Johnson, 1989) there are various reasons for this:

- Impairment of observation due to the distress caused by witnessing a crime
- Tendency to pay more attention to salient or dangerous aspects of the scene, such as a weapon
- Changes in recollection over time
- Differences in encoding and reporting context
- Suggestibility, especially in response to 'leading' questions.

Even given this inherent difficulty, eye-witness testimony is still one of the most important types of legal evidence.

Loftus' work suggests that there are two types of information involved. Information from the actual perception of the original event can be encoded, but so can information supplied after the event. It appears that the two become integrated (or, given the situation, perhaps 'confused' would be a more accurate word to use) and the witness is convinced that all the information is from one source. So leading questions by officials could add external information, and compound the problem.

If eye-witness testimony is so important, then, how might we improve it, given our theoretical knowledge about memory and forgetting? There are several ways in which researchers have suggested that forensic evidence might be clarified.

Cognitive Interviews

Fisher and Geiselman (1988) developed cognitive interview techniques involving retrieval mnemonics. These are mnemonic techniques which aid retrieval of traces rather than learning. There are four principles at work in a cognitive interview.

Encoding Specificity

If interviewers ask witnesses to reinstate the context in which the crime took place, they are recreating the encoding environment. This is the principle on which reconstruction of the crime is based, but the witness is doing this in his or her own mind rather than viewing a physical reconstruction.

Retrieval Paths

The police will often ask witnesses to tell them everything they can remember, even if the information appears to be unconnected, or unimportant. This is because doing so may open up new pathways to information during retrieval.

Order of Retrieval

Often more information can be retrieved when people are asked to recall in different orders than forwards chronologically. It appears that the most recent connection to information has the strongest trace, and then each piece of information acts as a retrieval cue to the previous event (Whitten and Leonard, 1981).

Role Play

Asking witnesses to take on the perspective of another person can often bring to light different information. Thinking about a crime from the victim's point of view can make the witness 'revisit' the scene.

The cognitive interview has been shown to be very useful in gaining more information from eye-witnesses, and improving the accuracy of the evidence. It does not, however, stop eye-witnesses from being brow-beaten by barristers.

State-dependent Forgetting

An interesting point to arise from eye-witness studies is that distress can alter recall of the event. Learning that takes place under the influence of certain classes of drugs is subsequently reproduced at better rates when the participants have been administered the same drugs, when compared to a drug-free state (see Overton, 1984). This pharmacological effect can be seen under other conditions, such as the physiological states associated with hunger and thirst, and time of day. Such studies were carried out in animals, but human experiments have shown similar state-dependent findings, including intoxication and drug-induced states (don't try this at home). This is also linked to the presence of appropriate cues, and appears to be even more important in states produced by changes in mood, rather than drugs. Poor recall rates have been observed when the mood at time of encoding is different from that at recall (Eich and Metcalfe, 1989). So in addition to contextual elements, there may be emotional elements to forgetting too.

Repression

Forgetting can sometimes be necessary. This can be because we need to replace information. Luria (1968) described a memory man who memorised so many long sequences of words or numbers for exhibition of his 'powers' that some were intruding on recall. He learnt to exert control over this. This type of forgetting is called motivated forgetting, but there is a kind of motivation other than the need to control feats of recall. Repression is the forgetting of painful or traumatic information. Freud (1915) would explain this as the need to defend the ego from conflict, and included the conflict caused by memories which are pleasurable, but immoral (1918). A man of his time if there ever was. He was also subject to this himself, as in the forgetting of the case of a 14-year-old girl suffering from stomach pains. Freud diagnosed a hysterical anxiety reaction, but the young girl died of stomach cancer. Freud then managed to forget all about the case, and stated that he had repressed the information. In the modern age of litigation it is unlikely that he would have been allowed to forget it so easily. For the Freud references see Strachey (1957). The evidence for repression, the recall of events under clinical conditions, and the subsequent alleviation of symptoms is suspect. Freud's theories are not possible to examine scientifically, which does not necessarily mean they are wrong, just not verifiable – a bit of a problem for Cognitive Psychology.

Amnesia

All of the theory and research detailed above refers to the everyday phenomenon of forgetting, the kind that happens to everyone. There is another kind, which has more serious implications for the individual: amnesia. The fictional representation of the amnesiac is misleading, so let us examine the real enigma of amnesia.

Classification of Amnesia

There are two basic forms of amnesia: *anterograde* amnesia is the inability to acquire new information, and *retrograde* amnesia is the inability to recall past events. Much of the research carried out in amnesia involves case studies. Each case of amnesia is unique, due to individual patterns of brain damage or psychological trauma (see the section on causes of amnesia), and psychologists or neurologists study such individuals in relation to the theoretical models of memory, etc. As the studies are based on individuals, each person is referred to in terms of their initials only.

Anterograde Amnesia

Probably the best-known case of anterograde amnesia is HM, who underwent some rather heavy-handed treatment for epilepsy including removal of the hippocampus (this occurred during the 1950s: see Penfield and Milner, 1958). The epilepsy diminished, but HM no longer had the ability to remember anything that had happened since the operation. Nothing. HM remembered his life before the operation, and could rehearse items, but they no longer transferred to any kind of permanent store. The poor man spent the rest of his life in an institution.

Wilson (1987) studied a patient, CM, who was recovering from the successful treatment of a malignant tumour in the left temporal lobe. CM could remember the names of his wife and children, etc., but could not learn new information. Anterograde amnesia is attributed to the failure to store information rather than retrieve it. Such phenomena are thought to provide further evidence for distinct transient and permanent stores.

Retrograde Amnesia

The two forms of amnesia can be distinguished. Sometimes they occur together; often they are separate. Retrograde amnesia means that the sufferer can no longer recall items prior to the event that was the source of the problem. Older memories may be intact, and the patient can acquire new memories.

Many amnesiac patients have other cognitive functions wholly or partially intact. The Swiss neurologist Claparede (cited by Schachter *et al.*, 1990) had a patient who could never recall meeting him. One day he shook hands with the patient, concealing a needle in his hand, pricking her. Next time he met her, she did not remember him, but hesitated when shaking hands. Some form of encoding had taken place, but not the memory of the neurologist.

It appears that there are highly specific impairments to one or other different kinds of memory. Skills might be retained from before the amnesiac event, such as in Schachter's (1983) case study MT. MT could play golf, and therefore utilise his procedural memory, but could never remember where the golf ball had gone. This indicates impairment to episodic memory. Obviously Schachter's ethical code prevented cheating on the golf course, and presumably MT still enjoyed a round. Tulving and Schachter (1990) studied KC who again had no memory of his past. If on one occasion he was given a phrase, he would be unable to recall it, but he could reconstruct it.

So there seem to be deficits produced in different stages of learning, encoding (as in HM and CM), storage and retrieval. There also appear to be as many patterns and outcomes of amnesia as there are individuals suffering from it. Why are there so many different observable deficits, and why do they happen?

Causes of Amnesia

The memory loss described above is attributable to two basic states – psychogenic (or functional) and organic. Psychogenic states mean that the amnesia is due to some psychological or psychiatric difficulty; organic means that there is a brain dysfunction, of whatever cause.

Psychogenic States and Amnesia

Negative life events are often associated with amnesia. Psychogenic or functional amnesia is a symptom of a dissociative disorder, which essentially means a loss of identity. There are various degrees of this form of amnesia.

Dissociative amnesia is an inability to recall specific information. Freud would term this repression (see above) as the information can be retrieved under certain circumstances, such as the injection of sodium pentothal (the 'truth drug' beloved of thriller writers). Most of the examinable evidence in this area (as opposed to that found by psychoanalysis) comes from combat zones. Post-traumatic stress disorder (PTSD) is a set of symptoms exhibited following traumatic events, such as being bombed to within an inch of your life. It used to be called shell-shock. PTSD sufferers do show highly specific memory loss along with anxiety and insomnia (McNally *et al.*, 1995).

Dissociative fugue is a disorder in which the amnesia is more complete, although it may be transient. This situation is the individual wandering the streets unable to remember who he or she is, and who may adopt a new identity. Schachter *et al.* (1982) studied PN, found wandering with no identification and no recollection of his identity. The fugue state cleared eventually after certain things happened to allow him to recall his life and himself, but he never recovered memory of the time during the fugue state.

Dissociative identity disorder is often called the multiple personality dis-order. This has become confused in the public's mind with other types of mental illness, and even possession. Due to the association with drama and prurient interest in such cases, it is difficult to accept the existence of this disorder. Many would say that it is manufactured by psychiatrists who have an interest in maintaining that the condition is a real one (Seltzer, 1994).

Perhaps they are right – there have been several books written on the case studies and hence a few reputations made. However, the majority of these case studies have turned out to be fake, people seeking attention by exhibiting several alter egos, or attempting to evade prosecution for serious crimes by shifting blame to another personality. Some do appear genuine, and are often associated with the need to deal with serious and sustained traumatic events, such as sexual abuse.

Psychogenic amnesia is still poorly understood, as with many psychiatric disorders. Why trauma affects some individuals in this way, and not others, is a question remaining to be answered.

Organic Amnesia

Loss of memory can also be associated with brain dysfunction. This can be transient or permanent. Head injuries and other temporary damage to the brain, such as that caused by epileptic fits or ECT, can result in temporary amnesia. Permanent organic amnesia has a wide range of causes, such as serious head injury, strokes, tumours, several nutritional conditions and some diseases.

> accident, alcohol and Alzheimer's three items associated with permanent organic amnesia – the three As. These are by no means the only causes of amnesia, but are examples of the three classes of problem: trauma to the head, nutritional disorders, and degeneration due to illness

Accident

Trauma to the head, caused either by accident of some form or because of psychosurgery, can be associated with permanent amnesia. See the cases cited above of patients HM and CM. Closed-head injury victims (being hit without penetration of the skull) also exhibit amnesia, but this is often accompanied by other problems. Cerebro-vascular incidents (strokes) mean that there has been disruption to the blood supply in the brain, and again sufferers can have resultant amnesia. There are also many cases of introduction of foreign objects into the brain which have resulted in memory loss. Most of the cases of injury or stroke who are then amnesiac appear to have damage in the temporal or frontal lobes.

Alcohol

In 1881 two neurologists, working independently, were studying patients suffering from severe conditions including profound memory loss and inability to acquire new information. Wernicke's encephalopathy, named after one of them, is a condition in which patients experience memory disturbance and confusion. Korsakoff was studying patients in which this condition was shown as a result of chronic alcohol abuse. The condition became known as Wernicke–Korsakoff syndrome, usually abbreviated to Korsakoff's syndrome. Korsakoff's syndrome is the condition resulting from degeneration of various parts of the brain caused by Wernicke's encephalopathy resulting from alcoholism. This causes thiamine deficiency, leading to haemorrhage in the grey matter of the brain. The resultant memory disorder is variable, but there is extensive retrograde amnesia. Wernicke's encephalopathy can be the result of things other than alcohol abuse, for example malnutrition, but sadly, patients with the alcoholic version of Korsakoff's syndrome are not difficult to find. A sobering thought, perhaps? If you are interested in knowing more about Korsakoff's syndrome, you are directed to Kopelmann (1995) and Beaumont *et al.* (1996).

Disease

There are several infections which can lead to brain damage, for example a viral infection of herpes simplex encephalitis. Lesions can form in the temporal lobe and hippocampus, again resulting in severe memory disorder.

Degenerative conditions, although not classed in the same way as infections, can be regarded as pathological states. Dementia means the decline in cognitive function associated with degeneration in brain structures. Probably the best-known form of dementia is Alzheimer's disease. Whilst most of us are unlikely to encounter amnesiac patients with severe head injuries, or even Korsakoff's syndrome, it is estimated that 6% of the over 65s suffer from Alzheimer's, and it is not restricted to this age group. Many of us will have to confront this condition at some time.

Memory impairment in Alzheimer's affects episodic memory most severely, with sufferers unable to properly encode experiential information. There is also 'intrusion' into memory, meaning that false information is often produced during recall. There are other forms of dementia associated with memory disorders, but with significant differences of their form.

So, there are several forms, and several causes of amnesia. They can, in certain cases, be treated, but the neuropsychologist needs to identify the amnesia first. There are several different types of assessment, and in the final section of this chapter we will briefly examine them.

Assessing Memory Disorders

The measurement of psychological functioning is known as psychometrics. Much of psychometrics grew out of the assessment of intelligence. A more

---
psychometrics the measurement of mental characteristics using standardised tests
---

detailed discussion of this can be found in Chapter 11. Some intelligence tests have been altered in order to assess memory, and there is a Wechsler Memory Scale (Wechsler, 1987). However, most clinicians working in amnesia agree that these tests are only partly useful, and other, specific tests have been devised. The allied tests are those designed to assess cognitive impairment.

Retrograde amnesia is the more difficult to assess, as it involves memories the patient once had and the assessor would not necessarily have knowledge of them. There is also the unevenness of the memory loss. Personal histories can be a useful way of assessing memory, but are time consuming and subject to *confabulation*. Auto-biographical cueing procedures get patients to recollect specific experiences in response to single word cues, but are still open to confabulation. A development of this by Kopelmann *et al.* (1990) is the autobiographical memory interview (AMI). Instead of asking personal recollections, the patient must recognise faces, recall events, etc. (that everyone should know), and there are sets of questions relating to childhood, young adulthood and recent times. Another form of assessment is memory questionnaires. An important aspect of amnesia is the impact it has on the patient's life, as often there is little or no insight into the memory loss. Asking relatives to complete the questionnaire, as well as the patient, is very useful. Some questionnaires even attempt to access *metamemory*, the knowledge we have about our memory.

> **confabulation** a tendency to fabricate answers or stories due to the production of a false memory, often after frontal lobe damage

Memory loss is also rarely found in isolation, and the assessment of other cognitive and neuropsychological functions is often useful.

Improving Memory

Whilst the treatment of amnesia should be left to the realm of psychiatry, there are several commonsense aids which are applicable to those of us who are not amnesiac, but just simply want to improve our memory. Labels, signs, diaries, are all things we use to help remember. Routines are helpful: how long into a new semester do you take to learn your timetable, for example? Going to the same place every week, and seeing the same lecturer (but hopefully not hearing the same lecture!) does make for memorisation.

There are various strategies employed to improve memory, in addition to the cues above. Mnemonics are strategies for organising and remembering information. Several types of mnemonic strategy are as follows:

- ► *Imagery* – associating a particular image with something you need to remember. The best-known type is the *method of loci* which involves the imaginary placement of items to be remembered. For example, to remember a shopping list, you might think of a milk bottle on the doorstep, apples in a bowl on the table, a loaf of bread on the chopping board, etc.
- ► *Acronyms* – phrases designed from the first letter of words in order to remember other words. For example, 'Richard Of York Gave Battle In Vain' gives the letters ROYGBIV and the colours of the rainbow: Red, Orange, Yellow, Green, Blue, Indigo, Violet.
- ► *Acrostics* – the reduction of information as in acronyms, but forming a real word. When diagnosing anxiety disorders, for example, clinicians must remember a fairly long list of symptoms to identify, or rules,

including eliminating an organic disease and psychosis. The acrostic for this is STOMACH:

Scanning and vigilance
Two or more worries
Organic disease (rule out)
Motor tension
Anxiety unrelated
Course of mood or psychotic (rule out)
Hyperactive autonomics

All these mean something specific to the person diagnosing (Short *et al.*, 1992).

There are several other strategies for improving memory, but I can't remember them.

We have looked at several theories of forgetting and the problems it can cause. 'Everyday' forgetting appears to be associated with either interference from information or the weakening of links and cues. Amnesia, on the other hand, is a more serious form of forgetting that can have traumatic or organic causes. Memory is therefore dependent on both good health and good organisation of information. In the next few chapters we will look at how information is organised and utilised.

Summary

There are two aspects of forgetting which we can study in psychology. 'Everyday' forgetting is that loss of information we all experience. This can be due to information decay, poor encoding or failure of retrieval links. There are several ways in which we can improve memory depending on why forgetting is happening. Mnemonic strategies, for example, improve encoding, whereas cognitive interviews for eye-witnesses attempt to reconstruct information already encoded, and improve retrieval. Amnesia, on the other hand, is a true dysfunction of memory, associated with psychological or physical trauma.

There are differences in the classification of these two forms of forgetting, and also in the study of them. Forgetting tends to be examined as a laboratory phenomenon, whereas amnesia is studied via case studies.

Memory has been studied extensively by cognitive psychologists. It is the part of the cognitive system that stores and retrieves information. It must also organise it, for efficient retrieval. The next chapter will examine the theories and research that suggest the ways in which information might be organised.

Self-test Questions

1 What are the two theories of everyday forgetting?
2 What is the difference between retroactive and proactive inhibition?
3 What are the traumas with which amnesia is associated?
4 What is the difference between anterograde and retrograde amnesia?
5 What are the differences in the ways in which forgetting and amnesia are studied?
6 Why do these differences occur?

CHAPTER 9

Organisation of Knowledge

Key terms

clustering model a model of knowledge representation in which concepts are stored together

cognitive economy a feature of models in which items are stored with lack of redundancy

declarative knowledge factual knowledge

internal lexicon the mental dictionary

particular affirmative a feature of sets in which portions of categories are included

proactive inhibition old material interfering with new

procedural knowledge knowledge about how to do things

production systems mental systems in which the knowledge is stored as production rules

productive knowledge knowledge based on production systems

propositional models models in which knowledge is stored as propositions

propositions the smallest components of knowledge which can stand alone

schemata, frames and scripts forms of knowledge storage and representation

semantic feature comparison model knowledge representation in which words become sets of features and members are compared

semantic network models hierarchical models of knowledge representation comprising nodes and attributes

semantic priming the phenomenon in which presentation of one word will bring about recall of related words

set-theoretical model a type of clustering model in which categories and attributes are stored together

spreading activation the presentation of one item held in a semantic net will trigger the activation of the net close by

universal affirmative a feature of sets in which all members of a category are included

Key names

Anderson • Bower • Collins and Quillian • Conrad • Foss • Meyer • Squire

In the last few chapters we examined how information might reach memory, and how it might be stored. In this chapter we will look at the organisation of material in more detail, and the next chapter will examine how we go about utilising that organisation. Our concern here then is to examine *knowledge representation*.

Knowledge Representation

Knowledge is organised information, that can be utilised in particular ways. A great deal of Cognitive Psychology has concentrated on this area, specifically the representation of semantic knowledge. This is because language and its use is highly developed and we can access and study semantic information. Thus the Cognitive Psychological approach to mental representation has concentrated on the *internal lexicon* or our mental dictionary. Words derive worth from the concepts they represent, and studying the way we retrieve and use them means we can learn about content, structure and process.

The ways in which we can study organisation tend to be laboratory based, although there are some more ecologically valid techniques we can use. One particular phenomenon, which has been examined minutely, is the tendency for the access of one lexical item to lead to the efficient access of semantically related items. This is known as *semantic priming* (Foss, 1982). For example, if you are presented with the word *bread* then there is a high probability that you will think of the word *butter*. This is the basis of a psychoanalytic technique called free association, but this would be useless unless there were some associations that were common to us all. The psychoanalytical technique is designed to identity aberrations in this commonality. Cognitive Psychologists are more interested in why we all have associations. There are several theoretical explanations for, and models proposed to describe, this semantic organisation. Many of these theories were influenced by the work of Bower. Looking at free recall studies, Bower proposed that the semantic organisation of memory was in the form of hierarchy, and this in turn has led to several ideas, including the clustering model, the semantic feature comparison model and network models.

Clustering Model

We have already discussed the clustering model briefly. The basis of this model is that concepts tend to be clustered together, so that memories for one dog are stored with that for all other dogs and so on. A development of this idea is the *set-theoretical model*. Here, not only are the members of a category stored together, but also their attributes. Retrieval from the groups of these members, attributes and associations involves a search through several sets to find overlap. So in order to find the answer to the question 'is a poodle a dog?' the attributes of the set 'dog' are compared with those of 'poodle', and the greater the overlap, the more easily the statement is verified or the answer found. This is measured by reaction time. There are two types of relations: a universal affirmative (AU), and a particular affirmative (PA). AU means that all members of one category are included in another ('all poodles are dogs'), whereas PA means only a portion are included ('some animals are dogs'). Such relations are important in the use of logic. Meyer (1983) proposed that there were two stages to the verification process. If there is no intersection in the sets, then a negative decision can be made quickly. But if there is an intersection, then a second stage is needed to determine the extent of the match. So 'all dogs are cats' leads to a quick negative decision, but 'all animals are dogs' is slower because there is an intersection. This is mediated by the size of the sets involved. However, it does not account for the difference in response when some members of the set are more typical than others. For example, 'a pigeon is a bird' is responded to much quicker than 'an ostrich is a bird'. A development of the clustering model called the set-theoretical model attempts to explain this.

Semantic Feature Comparison Model

Smith *et al.* (1974) suggested that words are represented as sets of semantic features. So each word has critical defining features, and characteristic features. The defining features are those that determine set membership (birds have wings, fly, have two legs, etc.) and characteristic features are those describing the particular example (pigeons are small and brown and coo a lot). When an atypical member such as the ostrich is found, then there are only some defining features that apply, and another piece of information must be brought into use. Also, there are some items that appear to conform to the set, that don't. Is a bat a bird? It flies, it has two wings, and two legs, but we know from other information that it does not belong to the set 'birds'. So there are different levels of comparison available. A major criticism of this model, though, is that defining features cannot have absolute properties. No single feature makes a bird, or not a bird.

These two models do enhance our properties of organisation, but cannot attempt to explain the larger issues of knowledge. There are more general theories of semantic memory, which come under the heading of network models.

Semantic Network Models

Semantic networks were briefly described in Chapter 7. Collins and Quillian (1969) developed the idea when looking at memory organisation of a computer program. They were working on the program called Teachable Language Comprehender (TLC), which was designed to understand text, and add new concepts from the text into its memory. The network envisaged in this way represented knowledge as nodes and attributes in a hierarchical structure. The value of such a representation is that it has *cognitive economy*, as attributes that are more general do not need to be stored with every member of a category. The model also incorporates intersecting searches and inheritance hierarchies.

Figure 9.1 is another example of how items might be stored in the Collins and Quillian model. Here 'canary' is stored with the information that it is yellow and can sing, but at a higher node it is also stored with the attributes of a bird, and even higher still, with the attributes of an animal. Thus there is no redundancy in storage. It can be tested by measuring the time it takes participants to search for and validate the properties of individual items. The number of levels that you need to search through increases the response time. This is an undeniable and easily verifiable finding. But there are problems with this elegant representation. Firstly, not every word or concept has a clearly defined set of attributes, so the hierarchical structure fails there. Also, there is the issue of categorical similarity. To determine that ostrich and canary are in the same category is quite quick; after all, it is only one step up the hierarchy to 'bird'. But suppose you were asked if 'canary' and 'elephant' were in the same category. According to the cognitive economy of storage it should take a long time, involving steps up and down the hierarchy. But if you try it in the laboratory, chances are it won't take your participants long to say canaries and elephants don't belong in the same category! This cannot be

Figure 9.1 *Collins and Quillian's hierarchical model of semantic memory: a further example*

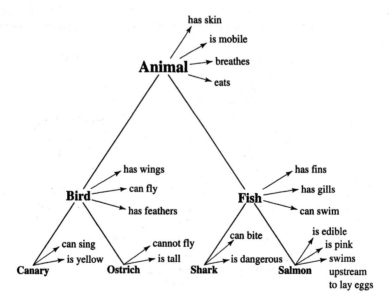

predicted by the Collins and Quillian model (Schaeffer and Wallace, 1970). Finally the model would predict that it would take longer to say a canary can fly, than to verify it can sing, as 'can fly' is stored up the hierarchy. This difference is not the case. Conrad (1972) attempted to account for this by examining the strength of the links between words and their properties. High and low frequency sentences such as 'a canary can sing' (high frequency) and 'a salmon has a mouth' (low frequency – well, how many times have you heard people talk about a salmon's mouth?) should take the same processing time. Again this is not the case, and Conrad concluded that the non-redundancy issue of storage was not in play and cognitive economy could not be happening. The model had to be modified to account for these findings, that linear searching up and down the hierarchy does not seem to happen (canary–elephant), and that there appears to be some difference in associative strength within links. Collins and Loftus (1975) therefore proposed a theoretical development known as the spreading activation theory.

Spreading Activation

In spreading activation, concepts are held in a conceptual space, linked by association to related concepts. Figure 9.2 shows a possible representation for the concept of 'sky' and its links. Spreading activation through the net means that as one item is triggered, those close by are also triggered. Showing the word 'sky' will trigger 'blue', 'aeroplane', 'cloud', etc. very quickly, and with a bit more time, 'green', 'pilot' and 'rain' will be found. As each word is activated, the activation spreads throughout the network. The extent of activation depends on the strength of the links between the initially activated node and the others. This could account for semantic priming, in which a word/concept becomes more accessible after a probe is presented.

Figure 9.2 *Spreading activation for the concept of 'sky'*

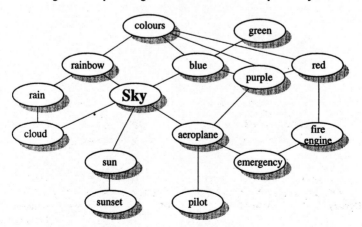

The only problem with this theory is how complicated it is, and it still doesn't give a realistic picture of organisation. It does explain those very strange links you can suddenly experience, however.

Another difficulty with semantic network models of this nature is, simply, that they describe only words and meanings and links between them. An alternative to these purely semantic networks is the propositional network models.

Propositional Networks

Rather than representing knowledge as single words, as the semantic networks do, propositional networks represent it in terms of propositions. Propositions are the smallest components of knowledge that can stand alone as meaningful units. Anderson and Bower (1973) developed this theory of knowledge representation into a model known as Human Associative Memory (HAM). This is a basic model in which knowledge is represented as propositions that are statements or assertions about the world. These are usually represented as subject–predicate constructions. For example, 'this cat is white' has as its subject 'this cat' and its predicate 'is white'. In HAM this would be represented by the components descending from a fact node, as in Figure 9.3. The representation of a more complex sentence, 'during the night in the park the hippie touched the debutante' (one that Anderson and Bower used), is shown below that. It has additional elements of Time, Location and Context with Fact being the statement component. When a verb is added in addition to the predicate, the Relation and the Object branches are also added. Branches are joined by conceptual nodes representing ideas and the

Figure 9.3 *Anderson and Bower's Human Associative Memory (HAM) model*

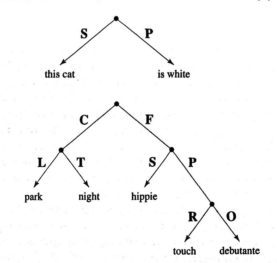

association between them. The conceptual nodes are present in memory before the sentence is encoded.

This model was developed further into ACT (adaptive control of thought). ACT includes three types of representation. *Working memory* is an active short term store containing the information currently available, including that retrieved from long term. *Declarative representation* is the factual knowledge we have and *productive representations* are like procedural knowledge, but comprise *production systems*. The productions in a system can be as complex as necessary, and can represent strings (the order of items), spatial images or abstract codes. For a more detailed description read Anderson (1996).

> production system sets of condition–action pairs called productions. A condition is, for example, an IF statement specifying a condition and an action is a THEN statement

Connectionist Models

An alternative to the network models discussed above comes from connectionist theory. In the semantic and propositional networks, for all their differences, knowledge is thought of as being stored as objects and the links between them. Connectionist models store the connection strength between items, which means that the storage is less localised, and patterns are evoked rather than found. This is based on the concept of the low-level neural storage, which is distributed in a parallel format. However, the models do not attempt to model the brain completely; the researchers simply say that this is closer to how the brain works.

Neurocognitive Evidence for Knowledge Representation

Learning and experience change the structure of the nervous system. The debate here is whether those changes are related to a localised or distributed storage of knowledge. Squire (1986) has made studies at a neural level, which led him to conclude that knowledge is in a localised storage, seeming to contradict equipotentiality. But Squire suggested that the processing of complex information might be distributed, with the more minute pieces of knowledge making up the complex level being accessed at the neuronal level. Amnesiac patients, for example, are deficient in episodic memory, but retain skills. This has led Squire *et al.* (1990) to propose that there is a taxonomy of knowledge representation such as that in Table 9.1.

Such a structure proposes that not only might there be differences in the neural storage of knowledge, but also differences in conscious and unconscious memory. This can explain the priming phenomenon. The perception of the word 'sky' is enhanced by presentation of 'blue' before it. 'Sky' is

Table 9.1 *Taxonomy of knowledge representation proposed by Squire* et al. *(1990)*

Declarative knowledge		Non-declarative knowledge			
Semantic	Episodic	Skills	Priming	Dispositions	Non-
Facts	Events	Motor	Perceptual	Simple	associative
		Perceptual	Semantic	classical	Habituation
		Cognitive	Shifts in	conditioning	Sensitisation
		Adaptation	judgement	Operant	
		level	and	conditioning	
			preference		

stored in episodic memory, but the link with 'blue' is procedural and more unconscious.

Summary

There are several models of knowledge representation each with its own format. Semantic network models contend that concepts are organised in units linked in a hierarchical representation of successively more general attributes, whereas propositional models represent knowledge as small units of meaningful information navigated by rules. Connectionist models represent knowledge as the strength of links, in which patterns are evoked, rather than found by activating searches. Neurocognitive evidence is unclear, but connectionist models appear to be closer to how the brain works.

Self-test Questions

1 How would semantic priming be explained by the three major types of knowledge representation models – semantic, propositional and connectionist?
2 Draw a propositional model representation of the idea of 'computer'.
3 How would spreading activation work in your model?

Information Use

This part examines how we use the highly organised knowledge structures described in the last chapter. Using the concepts we have acquired requires the application of reasoning in order to make decisions and solve problems, and the evidence of that reasoning is in measured intelligence and exhibited skill. The way we express that is by using language. The next few chapters will explore those issues.

CHAPTER 10

Thinking – Logic, Decision Making and Problem Solving

Key terms

concepts representations of items based on grouping by common attributes
decision making the process of making a choice between several alternatives based on the attractiveness and utility of each alternative
deductive reasoning reasoning based on sets of rules and logical relations between items
exemplar an example of a member of the concept which is the most typical
inductive reasoning reasoning based on prior experience and beliefs
mental models mental representations of the world and its state
problem solving a process directed towards finding a solution when no method is readily available
prototype a typical instance of a concept, the 'average'
syllogisms sets of logical statements

Key names

Bruner, Goodnow and Austin • Duncker • Hayes • Johnson-Laird • Medin • Meyer • Payne • Rosch • Tversky and Kahneman • Wertheimer

Having acquired, stored and organised information, we have to use it. Traditionally the processes of thinking and reasoning have been thought to be the end of the chain of information processing, as if they were the most sophisticated or mature processes that happen to material. This might be misleading. Perception, attention and memory have been thought to be closely allied to neural activity, and therefore viewed as more fundamental and basic. However, the more abstract theories of these cognitive activities do demonstrate that they can be thought of as higher processes in the same way as thinking can. Also, there is no reason to suppose that a neural model of thinking cannot be built. This chapter explores the theories and research in thinking and information use, and the following chapter will look at how these might manifest themselves in individuals.

When we looked at knowledge representation, it was almost as if we were considering static structures around which some kind of activity reverberates. However, thinking is an active process requiring manipulation of mental representations already stored and/or retrieved in order to form new representations, and it results in pieces of behaviour that can be measured. These representations are in the form of concepts, propositions, mental models, schemata and words and images.

Mental Representations

Concepts are representations that include the important properties of a class of objects or ideas (instances). The functions of concepts include:

▶ *Classification*: does an instance belong to the concept, subset, etc.?
▶ *Understanding*: classification allows information to be 'chunked' into meaningful units and hence bring prior knowledge to use on the current situation.
▶ *Prediction*: the access of knowledge in order to decide what to do in terms of predicting the following events.
▶ *Reasoning*: the access of information to provide inferential outcomes.
▶ *Communication*: sharing concepts means that people can communicate indirect experience.

For example, we might encounter a creature unfamiliar to us, but because of certain attributes we know it is a bird (classification), we know that it will fly (understanding) and that if we make sudden movements it might fly away (prediction), and we can tell someone else about this new bird we have seen without explaining that it was small, had wings, etc.

Learning concepts is the fundamental basis of cognitive development, and we continue to acquire them throughout our cognitive life.

Artificial concepts can be clearly defined. Such a concept is that of 'square', defined as a shape with four equal sides and four right-angled corners. Owing to the accessibility of artificial concepts they have been used to study concept formation. The major work in this was by Bruner *et al.* (1956). Their experiments involved arbitrary sets of images defined by several dimensions (colour, shape, etc.). The stimuli were cards with figures on them, which varied in terms of number, colour and type of shapes on the cards. There were up to three shapes which could be squares, circles or crosses, they could be red, green or black, and there could be a variable number of borders around the edges of the cards. In order to train their participants to learn the concept, Bruner *et al.* used either:

▶ a selection paradigm, in which participants selected cards and asked for classification, or
▶ a receptive paradigm, in which participants were shown cards by the experimenter and asked to give classification, and were then given feedback as to correctness.

The selection paradigm was an active hypothesis-testing situation. Participants were not told what the concept was; they simply had to learn whether or not cards conformed to it. A limited number of strategies for deciding on the concept were identified.

Natural concepts, on the other hand, cannot be so clearly defined. The concept 'bird' has instances included that do not conform to all the attributes. Ostriches cannot fly, for example, but bats can. Ostriches are definitely birds, though, and bats do not belong to this class at all. Natural concepts are known as 'fuzzy' in that the boundaries are moveable. There are some instances, though, that are typical of a concept. Think about 'bird': what image do you have? This is known as a *prototype*. While most instances share the prototype qualities, not all have all attributes. The concept therefore is made up of more than the prototypical attributes; it also has a *core*, the properties that are most important for membership.

There are three major theories about concept formation involving such findings:

▶ *Prototype theory.* The prototype theory of concept formation proposes that we look for commonality amongst items. When this is found we group the items together, and common features are abstracted and stored as a schema. New information can be compared with the schema, and categories are formed. The prototype is the best description of a category, but is not necessarily a real item (Rosch, 1975).

▶ *Attribute theory.* This theory suggests that we look for the defining features (attributes) of an item. Medin (1989) proposed that we form mental lists of the attributes and compare new items with the list. But it is not always possible to specify the defining features, nor does it account for *exemplars*.

▶ *Exemplar theory.* Exemplars are similar to prototypes, but instead of being a 'summary representation' they are particular items which best represent the concept. So where the prototype of 'bird' is an image of some creature with wings, feathers, in a nest perhaps, etc., the exemplar is an actual bird which is most representative, perhaps a sparrow (Medin and Shoben, 1988). It is likely that this is the way children use concepts, as they have not encountered many examples.

The storage of concepts is likely to be as one of the structures discussed in Chapter 9. As we learn more, we can combine concepts. Relating concepts together is achieved by using propositions. For example, we have a concept for dogs, and one for cats; a proposition about them might be that dogs chase cats.

Mental models, on the other hand, are propositions about how things work, or representation of abstract concepts (Johnson-Laird, 1988). When these are incorrect, we learn a great deal about behaviour. For example, an incorrect mental model about illness may lead to the incorrect use of medication. Reasoning based on mental models is essentially a semantic process. Inferences are made when a model is constructed which represents all the *premises* to be included. The following example will demonstrate.

Premises:
   The light-bulb is to the right of the pad
   The pen is to the left of the pad
   The mail is in front of the pen
   The butterfly is in front of the light-bulb

Conclusion:
   The mail is to the left of the butterfly

If you don't believe me, look at Figure 10.1. According to Johnson-Laird, we construct a mental model, either a pictorial one such as in the figure, or a verbal/spatial one:

PEN	PAD	LIGHT-BULB
MAIL		BUTTERFLY

This makes it easier to arrive at the conclusion. More than one model may be needed, or may be specified by the premises.

Mental models rely on the capacity of working memory, and a more graphical representation may be taking more capacity. Also, the more models that are consistent with the premises, the more capacity is being used too.

Schemata are general basic knowledge units similar to mental models, but give rise to expectation. *Scripts* are schemata about familiar sequences of activities, and can help with processing normal events, but can slow us down or lead to inaccurate decisions when the unexpected happens.

We often translate ideas into words or images to assist with information processing, and these in turn can lead to the development of cognitive maps

Figure 10.1 *Illustration of mental model*

(see Chapter 12). These can be distorted and incomplete. For example, in your university or college, the buildings are probably designed so that the rooms next to each other are numbered consecutively, but what if one building is numbered so that one side of the building holds even-numbered doors and the odd-numbered doors are on the other side? You will probably wander round the building looking for a particular office or classroom for some minutes, because your prototypical concept gives a cognitive map which is inaccurate.

So these are the basic units of active knowledge. Let us look at how they might be used.

Logic

Many studies have considered logical thinking. *Deductive reasoning* involves finding the truth or falsity of conclusions based on logical relations. A basic unit of logic is the *syllogism*.

Syllogisms

Syllogisms are sets of statements which assert some fact, then allow an inference to be drawn. They are in the form

All A are B
All A are C

then you are left to conclude – what? All B are C? Well, that would not be quite accurate. Consider what happens when you add concrete ideas instead of A, B and C:

All cats are animals
All cats are furry

We cannot conclude that all animals are furry, firstly because we know that this is not the case (although this is not deductive), but also because the logical conclusion *cannot* follow from the statements.

Humans make many errors in logical reasoning of this nature. There are several reasons for this.

Bias
Consider the following statements:

1 Britain is free country.
2 In a free country, all people have equal opportunities.
3 Conclusion: therefore in Britain all people have equal opportunity.

The conclusion is valid logically, but agreement or disagreement is made because of *prior belief*, not because of the use of logic. This is very much the problem with stereotypes: logically valid arguments are often confounded by supposed knowledge.

Conversion Effect

It is often assumed that if A leads to B, then B leads to A. This is not so. Voting Conservative in British elections does mean that the voter has British citizenship, but does British citizenship mean that the voter will vote Conservative? Obviously not!

Limits on Working Memory

In order to follow logical assertions, particularly long ones or those involving negatives, we must hold a lot of information in memory. Logical errors occur if we are asked to do more than can be dealt with in the capacity of working memory.

We also see cultural differences in the use of logic. Anthropological studies of groups of people described as non-literate found that they would make perfectly reasonable conclusions, but that they were not basing them on logical rules. For example, Cole and Scribner (1977) found that the following exchange could take place:

> Mr Smith is a man
> All men live in this village
> Does Mr Smith live in this village?

The *logical* conclusion here is that, yes, Mr Smith does live in this village. However, the reply found was 'I do not know, I have never met Mr Smith'. This does suggest that the rules of formal logic are not necessarily part of the natural laws of thought. People appear inherently to treat problems of this nature as something which can be answered from observation. What then is the kind of reasoning that we use every day, if formal reasoning is not part of our experience?

Natural Reasoning

If deductive reasoning is the procedure of working through logical relations, then *inductive reasoning* is establishing a degree of belief in a hypothesis on the basis of observation. Again errors are made:

One friend had a bad experience with a Ford
Therefore, all Fords are unreliable.

This is plainly not a logical conclusion, but when weighing up evidence before spending money on a car, it might be one way of eliminating a particular make. (Apologies to Ford.)

One way of using reasoning effectively is to employ *heuristics*. For example, you are about to leave your house and you cannot find your keys. What do you do? A systematic search of all the rooms would be effective, and you would find your keys. You would also miss the bus. However, what about stopping and using past experience to predict where they might be? This would be using a heuristic, and might be effective. There is a trade-off between speed and accuracy. Heuristics often work well and can guide judgements. According to Kahneman and Tversky (1982) three types of heuristics are commonly employed.

> heuristic a 'rule of thumb' or device which limits the search for a solution in large problems

Anchoring

We often estimate the probability of an event, not from scratch, but based on some earlier event. For example, you originally thought that the probability of having your car stolen in a particular city was 90%. You are told by a reliable source that it is only 1%. You revise your estimate – to 80%!

This has direct effects in the legal system. In most Western countries the prosecution evidence is presented first. This means that the defence have a hard time, as juries are already convinced, at least partially.

Representativeness

We base the belief that something belongs to a larger class of items on similarities. If you meet a man who is tidy, wears glasses and speaks in a whisper, do you that assume he is a librarian, or a farmer? You will choose one profession, but a decision cannot really be made here. The decision is based on prior knowledge, and focusing on the level of representativeness rather than the amount of information actually available.

Availability

Judgements of the likelihood of an event are made on the basis of how easily examples are brought to mind. This can work well, but not always. Consider the television news. How often does it depict murders, muggings or airline crashes? They are not very frequent, but they are very memorable. This memorability can lead us to suppose that these types of events have high frequency, and therefore are highly likely to happen, hence the avoidance of city centres, particular airlines, etc.

So how do we use heuristics to make decisions and solve problems?

Decision Making

Decision making is about choosing between alternatives. There are two main classes of decision making models: *compensatory* and *non-compensatory*.

Compensatory Models

These model the fact that the decision-making process allows attractive dimensions of the alternatives to compensate for unattractive. Additive models arrive at a total score for each choice, and additive-difference models take the difference of the rating of dimensions between a new alternative and the first one evaluated, to arrive at a score (Table 10.1)

Table 10.1 *Additive and additive-difference compensatory models*

Dimension	Additive ratings		Additive-difference ratings		
	Choice A	Choice B	Choice A	Choice B	Difference
1	+1	+2	+1	+2	−1
2	−2	+3	−2	+3	−5
3	+3	−1	+3	−1	+4
4	+2	+2	+2	+2	0
Total	+4	+6			

In both models, choice B is the most attractive alternative. This is very systematic, but it is questionable whether people really use such processes while making decisions. If you have the choice of going out for the evening or finishing that essay, do you use this technique? Perhaps in group decisions, where the process must be overt and rigorous, such techniques are used, but then the decision is at a higher level of consciousness and observability.

Non-compensatory Models

These models allow for the elimination of alternatives from the whole system of judgement.

Elimination by aspects (Tversky, 1972) allows for the elimination of alternatives based on the sequential evaluation of their aspects. Certain minimum criteria must be satisfied to avoid elimination from the selection procedure. Aspects are evaluated in order of importance, this being determined by some sort of rating scale.

Conjunctive models also require that alternatives satisfy minimum criteria before being selected. However, each alternative is considered on (potentially) all dimensions before the next is satisfied. This is known as a *satisficing search* (Simon, 1957) in which people select a good alternative, i.e. one which satisfies the criteria.

The fundamental difference between the models is the way in which we search for the information. Payne (1976) used this point to identify the strategies used. Strategies are either *inter-dimensional* (evaluation of each alternative separately on all dimensions) or *intra-dimensional* (considering the comparison alternatives on single dimensions). They can also be either *constant* (same number of dimensions for all alternatives) or *variable* (elimination of some alternatives before all dimensions are considered).

According to Payne's work in problem solving, the tendency is to change strategy in accordance with the demands of the task. The heuristics for problem solving are adapted to the information processing demands of the task, in order to make an attempt to keep them within the capabilities of the individual. Studies in decision making also support such a hypothesis. For example, when one is faced with a large number of alternatives elimination by aspects or conjunctive strategies are used, but with a smaller number a more cognitively demanding strategy is used. Take, for example, a set of people faced with the task of appointing a new member of staff. Pre-interview short-listing can be seen as shortening the number of alternatives from many applicants to a few interviewees. It is unlikely with a large number of applicants that they will all be considered on all criteria. Short-listing is often carried out on a minimum criteria matching strategy. At interview, however, there are fewer candidates, and a more thorough search for criterion matching will take place (Gavin, 1992).

Incorporating conditions of uncertainty into decision making complicates matters. When deciding whether to go out or finish the essay, you might need to know what the penalties would be for late submission, or, indeed, what the probability of losing a friend by not attending her birthday party might be. Accurate probability estimates are therefore sometimes necessary for good decision.

Probability and Decision Making

The ability to make accurate estimates is a valuable skill, especially in risky decision making. Such decisions are those concerned with uncertainty, e.g. evaluating potential nuclear threats, medical diagnosis, buying insurance, etc. Our panel of interviewers selecting job candidates also have elements of uncertainty to weigh up, such as estimates of a candidate's honesty and potential loyalty, together with the ability to do the job.

Probability estimates are based on heuristics, which may or may not be accurate. Availability and representativeness may lead to the decision being erroneous, because relevant information may be unavailable or bias leads to inaccurate perception of the information. Anchoring may lead to an original unreliable decision not being reversed, with undesirable consequences.

The revision of estimates in the light of new evidence has been studied by the application of Bayes' Theorem. The amount of revision is derived as the ratio of the probability of two hypotheses after new data (D) has been added. This is calculated as the ratio of the original probabilities multiplied by the probability of obtaining the data if one or other hypothesis was true. This is quite complex, so here's the formula:

$$\frac{p(H_1/D)}{p(H_2/D)} = \frac{p(H_1)}{p(H_2)} \times \frac{(D/H_1)}{(D/H_2)}$$

This is best illustrated using an example. Suppose hypothesis 1 (H_1) is 'candidate A is honest', then this means hypothesis 2 (H_2) must be 'candidate A is dishonest'. Given an initial set of circumstances and data (the candidate's c.v.) the odds are 3:1 in favour of H_1. During the interview, it transpires that a chronological gap in the c.v. is due to the candidate having spent time in prison for tax evasion. These new data (D) give a likelihood of their appearance, if H_1 were true, as 1:100 000. The new odds (the revision) are 3:100 000, a probability of H_1 being true of 0.00003, very low.

In risky decision making, values are assigned to the dimensions in the same way as in the additive model. But also, the probability that something will occur must be assigned. The combination of such values and probabilities is described as *expected values*, the addition of the produce of value and probability. It would be feasible to assume that a high expected value would lead to decisions in favour of that alternative, but such predicted behaviour is not always the case. People often choose a negatively rated option such as continuing to gamble or smoke. Thus some alternatives can be seen to have *subjective utility*, allowing attractive aspects to make the expected value positive and even high. The probabilities are also subjective, and some dimensions are more influential.

So there appears to be less rationality in human decision making than would at first be thought, and heavy reliance on heuristics to reduce cognitive load at the expense of optimal decisions. This is not to suggest that decision making in this fashion is always flawed, but it might explain some of the problems that humans, as individuals and as a species, have created for themselves. A more optimistic view of human thinking might be found when we turn to problem solving.

Problem Solving

Problem solving is a directed process intended to find a solution when no obvious method is available. The solution is defined as the *goal state*. Problem solving as a process is completely internalised and the only ways we have of inferring what is going on are by making the internal processes explicit, or by observing behaviour. Let us consider two influential theories of problem solving, the Gestalt and information processing.

Gestalt Theory of Problem Solving

The Gestalt approach, using introspection, identified four stages in thinking about problems:

1 Preparation: information is gathered and initial attempts to reach the goal are made.
2 Incubation: the problem is set aside, and other activities are carried out.
3 Illumination: the solution appears in a flash of insight.
4 Verification: the solution is checked.

This being a Gestalt theory, and found by introspection, there is little evidence that this actually happens in all cases. However, a major contribution that this approach made is in the study of *functional fixedness*.

When participants were given three boxes with matches, candles and tacks and asked to fix a candle on a screen to make a lamp, Duncker (1945) observed that they found the task very difficult. However, half of the participants were given three empty boxes, with the candles, matches and tacks simply laid next to them, and they found the solution much more easily. The correct way to do it is to melt the base of a candle, and stick the candle to a box. The box is then fixed to the screen by the tacks. The first group, with the boxes filled, were in a *pre-utilisation* condition and the placing of the objects inside the box had fixed the function of the boxes as containers, and blocked the possibility of any other function. Prior experience had a negative effect on problem solving. There are situations, however, where prior experience has a positive effect, and practice with problems of this kind can lead people to use novel methods of solution finding (Meyer, 1983).

> functional fixedness the inability to perceive elements of a problem in a novel way due to prior experience (Duncker, 1945)

Gestalt theory states that problem solving is carried out by recombining or reorganising the elements of a problem. Wertheimer (1959) suggested that there are two kinds of thinking involved – *reproductive thinking* which simply reproduces old behaviour (things that have worked before) and *productive thinking* in which new organisations (Gestalts) are formed.

Information Processing

The information processing approach takes a different perspective. Newell and Simon attempted to use computer simulation to model human problem solving. They used the technique of *verbal protocols* to identify what human problem solvers do, then specified this information as computer programs.

> verbal protocols a technique in which human participants talk aloud about what they are doing and why, when performing a task such as solving a problem. These can be highly detailed and specific, if taken from a lot of people and made into a composite protocol

The outcome of this work was the General Problem Solver or GPS (Newell and Simon, 1963), a computer program which solves mathematical theorems. GPS is described in more detail in the chapter on machine 'thinking', but for now let us examine the findings of this approach.

There are three principal elements:

- the problem solver (the information processing system attempting to find a solution)
- the problem (the task environment)
- the problem representation (the problem space).

The problem solver has a number of strategies that can be used. These are facts, algorithms and heuristics. Facts are those things which are known without needing more cognitive energy than is required to retrieve them, e.g. 2 multiplied by 2 is 4, string can be used for tying things, etc. Algorithms are sets of rules and procedures which, if applied correctly, will always generate the correct outcome, e.g. multiplication rules or (one hopes) recipes. Heuristics, as already mentioned, are generalised strategies for carrying out tasks. Facts and algorithms can guarantee an answer; heuristics are more efficient, but will not always get the answer.

The task environment describes the type of problem encountered. Is it a mathematical question, a logic puzzle, or a physical task like Duncker's candles?

The problem state has been the major contribution that computer simulation has made to the area. It is the mental representation of the problem and comprises the initial state, the goal state, intermediate problem states and operators:

1 The initial state is the starting position.
2 The goal state is the position in which the problem has been solved, and there can be several potential goal states.
3 Intermediate states are steps along the way from initial to goal states.
4 Operators are possible moves. Operators can either change one state to another, or divide the goals into a series of sub-goals.

According to Hayes (1978) we use several strategies to navigate through the problem space:

1 Random trial and error means that operators are randomly chosen until the goal state is reached. This can be very wasteful.
2 Hill climbing means gradual movements from the initial to the goal state. From the position of the current state (which can be initial or intermediate) an evaluation is made of the state achieved by all possible moves, and the move that gets the problem solver closest to the goal is chosen. The difficulty here is that 'local highs' can be reached. Think about the activity from which the name is derived. In order to reach the summit of a hill it is possible to reach a subsidiary peak, which is higher than other possible places, and therefore near the goal, but has not achieved the desired end.
3 Means–end analysis is probably the most effective, but the most complex. The problem solver works on one goal at a time. If that cannot be the creation of the goal state, then it can be a sub-goal of removing

Figure 10.2 *The Towers of Hanoi problem*

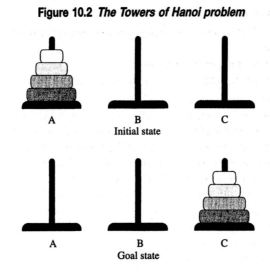

A   B   C
Initial state

A   B   C
Goal state

barriers. Procedures for achieving each goal are found, and these might result in moving further away from the goal state temporarily. One problem in which this has been successfully demonstrated is the Towers of Hanoi puzzle. In this there are three pegs with rings of different sizes placed on them (see Figure 10.2). The task is to move all the rings from A to C in the configuration shown, only moving one peg at a time, never placing a ring on top of another ring that is smaller, and only moving the top ring in any stack. Using a means–end analysis, the solution could be achieved by getting to states that appear to be further away from the goal. Try it.

Summary

It appears that people are quite similar in the way they think, make decisions and solve problems. There are some problems in researching this area, however, in that the verbalisation of thinking processes is quite difficult, and does not necessarily gain access to those processes. This makes it hard to achieve knowledge about thinking, and to simulate it. The observable behaviour can be simulated, however, and we will discuss this further in the chapter on machine thinking.

Self-test Questions

1 How do prototype and exemplar theories of concept formation differ?
2 How might you demonstrate how to overcome functional fixedness?
3 What is the difference between problem solving and decision making?

CHAPTER 11

Creativity and Intelligence

Key terms

accommodation modifying existing mental structures to fit reality
assimilation interpretation of events in terms of present mental structures
automatisation execution of mental processes with increasing efficiency
centration focusing on one striking feature of an object and ignoring others
conservation understanding of stability of properties of objects
creativity the ability to produce valued outcomes in a novel way
divergent thinking generation of multiple useful possibilities from a given situation
egocentrism being embedded in one's own point of view
equilibration balancing assimilation and accommodation
g general intelligence
IQ a measure of ability on tests which is calculated as the ratio of a measured
    mental age to chronological or actual age, multiplied by 100
psychometrics the study and use of standardised tests of ability and personality

Key names

Binet and Simon • Galton • Gardner • Piaget • Spearman • Sternberg (and Frensch)

In the last chapter we explored the idea that there are general patterns to thinking. One area where *differences* are seen, however, is in the output of thinking, the different levels of the property we call intelligence, and the likelihood of creative thought.

The study of intelligence has a relatively long history in psychology. Galton (1869) was interested in whether intelligence was inherited, and claimed that there was a strong innate component because families of outstanding people will produce others who are intelligent too. There is an immediately obvious problem with this argument, in that families share environments, and the similarity in intelligence, creativity or skill level might be due to environmental factors rather than genetic ones. This nature/nurture debate is one that is central to psychology, but nowhere is it more evident than in the studies of intelligence and creativity. The first thing we should examine, then, is how to recognise intelligence, creative thought or exceptional skill.

Defining and Measuring Intelligence

An early definition of intelligence was given by Binet and Simon (1905) who stated that it is the ability to judge, comprehend and reason well, together with good sense, the faculty to adapt and use initiative. It is obvious from reading other chapters in this book that this definition leaves more unsaid than it answers. The suggestion here is that intelligence comprises several components, and that there are several fundamental abilities inherent in it. Presumably to be intelligent, we must be able to make sense of all the information that reaches our sensory system, but it is evident that a disability in one sensory modality does not impair intelligence (Sternberg and Frensch, 1990). We must be able to organise and store information, and retrieve it effectively, but forgetting information does not mean lack of intelligence. The image of the absent-minded professor is too strong in our culture for that to be true. The relation of the fundamental abilities making up intelligence is difficult to determine. Spearman (1927) looked at scales measuring several abilities, such as reading comprehension, manipulation of numbers, etc., and found that people's scores on such scales were highly correlated. If they scored high on one test, then the likelihood was they scored high on others, and the same for low scorers. He suggested that this showed a general factor for intelligence, 'g', made up of several specific factors. This is known as the factor-analytic approach. As such this is purely psychometric and gives no cognitive explanation for intelligence. Spearman did suggest several qualitative and quantitative principles of cognition that were relevant to intelligence, but we had to wait for the information processing theorists to attempt a cognitive approach to intelligence studies.

Sternberg (1977) combined the psychometric approach with the more empirical approach, by looking at the relationship between intelligence as measured on the tests, and performance on complex cognitive tasks.

Measurement of intelligence is by means of mental tests, the so-called intelligence tests. The first documented use of such tests was by Catell in 1890, who was influenced by Wundt and Galton. However, it was Binet working with 'retarded' children who developed the first standardised tests for a variety of functions, culminating in the publication of the Binet–Simon tests of 1904–11. The modern equivalents of these tests lead to individual scores of intelligence quotients (IQ). It must be pointed out that this is a particular type of score, on a particular type of test, and is not a handy way of describing intelligence. Traditionally the IQ was the ratio of mental age (MA) to chronological age (CA) multiplied by 100:

$$IQ = \left(\frac{MA}{CA}\right) \times 100$$

If MA is equal to CA then the IQ is 100. This simple calculation is not the way in which IQ is found in modern tests, however, as there are problems with comparing across age groups. For a more detailed description of intelligence tests you are directed to Anastasi and Urbina (1997). For now, we will simply accept that there are tests that can access certain abilities with high reliability, and which test observable behaviour that we call intelligent. Many psychologists and others have criticised the IQ test, because it is a test of highly specific behaviour and does not access the cognitive components. Sternberg's tasks were of analogical reasoning, using an analytic technique to determine the stages of reasoning that participants were demonstrating. Analogical reasoning is the use of similarities between different situations that leads to further inferences. There was high correlation in Sternberg's studies, compared with Hunt's (1978) finding that there was little relation between measured intelligence and performance on simple tasks. It would seem that there needs to be something to 'stretch' the mind before such individual differences are seen.

There is still a problem here in examining intelligence as a cognitive function. Whilst the cognitivists claim that psychometric approaches are too narrow, they are still using psychometrically assessed intelligence as the criterion on which to compare cognitive tests. Perhaps this is a narrow definition and examination of intelligence. Gardner (1983) does suggest that instead of one intelligence made up of several components, there are several intelligences – linguistic, logical–mathematical, spatial, musical, kinaesthetic, interpersonal and intrapersonal – and that lack in one does not deny high levels of the others. For example, you might be tone-deaf, but still very intelligent in other areas, even if you are missing out on a lot. This still relies on measuring intelligence using suspect methods. Perhaps the major contribution to a cognitive understanding of intelligence is the study of its development.

Development of Intelligence

Cognitive development is the changes that occur to cognitive structures, abilities and processes during the life-span. The major theory in this area is the stage theory proposed by Piaget (1954).

Piagetian Stage Theory

From observations of children when he was working in the Binet laboratory, Piaget concluded that cognitive development consisted of the development of logical competence, due to the need to adapt to the world. Adaptation occurs through two processes: *assimilation* and *accommodation*. Piaget suggested that a schema is an organised pattern of thought or behaviour, such as the fact that babies will suck anything that will fit into the mouth, or when you walk into a lecture theatre you can immediately recognise the role of the person standing at the front. Also babies must accommodate new information in to the sucking schema, such as when presented with a cup. Your schema for 'lecturer' might be challenged if the person at the front is very young in comparison to other tutors. Assimilation and accommodation, then, must be balanced, and Piaget suggested new information causes cognitive dis equilibrium. *Equilibration* is the attempt to balance and lower disequilibrium. The processes are acting on internal operations – internalised, mental actions that manipulate, transform and return objects in a world to their original state. These three processes occur throughout life, but at various stages a different structure of thought is used to guide their action. There are four stages, which occur at approximately the same age in everyone, but again, there are wide individual differences.

> **assimilation** the interpretation of action or events in terms of existing structures of knowledge (schemata)
> **accommodation** the modification of schemata to fit new information

Sensorimotor Stage

Mental operations do not occur in very young children (birth to two years), according to Piaget, but they learn about the world by physical interaction. Thus a young child will reach out to grasp, or will throw, simply to experience the sensation and to observe what will happen. During this period, the major achievement is *object permanence* when a child will realise that objects exist even when not in sight. However, they remain completely *egocentric* which means that the world is viewed only from their perspective. Children up to five years, or sometimes more, are unable to imagine the view that a teddy bear has on the 'three mountain task'. Three mountains are placed on a table and a teddy bear is seated on one side, and the child on another. The egocentric child is unable to pick out from a series of pictures the view that the teddy bear is 'seeing'. This task has many criticisms, not least the fact that no one asked the children if they thought the teddy bear could see anything.

> **object permanence** up to about 12 months old, the removal of an object from a child's sight gives the child the impression that it has disappeared; after this age the child will actively look for objects when hidden. It now appears that aspects of object permanence are developed at around 4–5 months, but the full understanding appears later (Baillargeon and DeVos, 1991)
> **egocentricity** the tendency to view the world from one's own perspective. Note the child, when covering his or her eyes, says 'you can't see me!'

Pre-operational Stage

At around two years until 5–7 years children begin to develop symbolic thought, manifested by the use of language, imagery and categorisation. As a result, children can interact with those around them in a less physical way, and can construct solutions to problems without action. They remain egocentric, however, although there is evidence that Piaget's conclusions may have been erroneous here, and the task set to test it too complex.

Piaget also noted *centration* – the tendency to focus on one striking feature of an object. When choosing between two chocolate bars, for example, if one is long and the other thick, the pre-operational child will choose the long one, even though the amount of chocolate is the same.

Concrete Operational Stage

At about 7–12 years, children become able to operate internal representations of concrete objects. The major way of measuring the development of this stage is by experiments in *conservation*. Only when conservation of liquid quantity, number and mass are demonstrated has the child mastered concrete operations.

> **conservation** the knowledge that basic properties of objects or situations remain stable (are conserved) even though superficial qualities may change. Pouring water from a tall, thin beaker to a short, wide one, for example, means that there is still the same amount of water, but pre-operational children do not realise this. The conservation of liquid, number and mass is shown in Figure 11.1

At this stage too, they develop the concept of transitivity, i.e. if $a<b$ and $b<c$ then $a<c$. For example, pre-operational children cannot hold enough information in mind to solve the question: 'if Helen is taller than Joanne, and Joanne is taller than Alison, who is the shortest person?'. Younger children will pick Joanne or Alison, as each is shorter than someone else, and they cannot put the two pieces of information together. Children who have mastered concrete operations will choose the correct person. When asked about the two beakers, they will choose

Figure 11.1 *Conservation experiments to test child development*

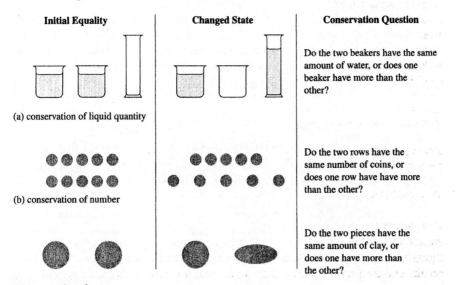

| Initial Equality | Changed State | Conservation Question |

(a) conservation of liquid quantity — Do the two beakers have the same amount of water, or does one beaker have more than the other?

(b) conservation of number — Do the two rows have the same number of coins, or does one row have have more than the other?

(c) conservation of mass — Do the two pieces have the same amount of clay, or does one have more than the other?

the correct option (the same amount of water) and justify it with 'you just poured it from one to the other'.

Formal Operational Stage

At around 12–15 children begin to think in more abstract terms. When asked to justify their answers on the conservation question, children in this stage will use a discussion of the law, or its application, to explain, rather than to say that they had watched the experimenter move the items. It is at this age that the ability to reason with abstract concepts and frame and test hypotheses appears. This has obvious implications for educational timetables: for example, when did you start to learn algebra, or formal science? It is also obvious that these experiments were carried out in the 1950s, as Piaget managed to get teenagers to participate in such odd activities.

Piaget's theory and findings are very important, and dominated the psychological field for many years. But there are some criticisms. For example, the theory depends on underlying logical structures for its idea of progression, but much of what we deal with every day is not bound by science or logic, so the theory may only apply to a set of cognitive processes. There is also too much emphasis on a linear progression through the stages, which may not reflect what really goes on in development. Some types of operations may be applicable at different times for different people, so that someone may be able to think in abstract terms about music or poetry, but still be in a concrete operational stage with respect to mathematical functions (a strange picture of an expert musician who is still using his or her fingers to work out change occurs here).

An alternative approach to cognitive development is supplied by information processing. Looking at the components of the cognitive system, information processing theorists examine how each changes with age. This allows us to gain a perspective that concentrates on continuous changes, rather than broader qualitative stages of Piagetian theory.

Information Processing

According to this approach, the basis of change is the growth of the knowledge base. The size of the general knowledge base is smaller in children, and grows with age, and this is not a function of memory capacity (Lindberg, 1980).

Automatisation of cognitive processes also increases as children grow, with younger children less able to divert attention away from sensorimotor tasks. Distract a young toddler whilst he or she is walking, and the result will be the same each time, but an older child will be able to talk to you. However, he or she will not be able to perform abstract tasks and high-level sensorimotor skills at the same time, which is why 12-year-olds are not allowed to drive!

The changes in the sophistication of cognitive strategies are also seen as a developmental progression. Younger children will, for example, use simple strategies to aid memory, such as rote repetition, but older children will use more elaborative strategies (Alexander and Schwanenflugel, 1994). The differences here can be seen not only from younger to older children, but across the age groups too. The individuals comprising a group of 5–6 year olds learning the times tables can exhibit rote learning of each multiplication, without understanding, or rote learning of each table, or an application of the extended addition rule.

One element of the information processing approach is the influence of *metacognition*. This means thinking about thinking, and refers to whether or not people understand how they perform cognitive tasks. Children develop this ability, and learn to regulate their thinking and develop a *feeling of knowing* (Costermans *et al.*, 1992), which young children do not experience.

Examining the development of intelligence in general ways like this gives us insight into the ways in which we use the information we store and retrieve. Another interesting approach to intelligence is to study individuals who exhibit extremes of behaviour within the definition. In addition to retardation and learning difficulty, and the opposite end of the spectrum, giftedness, one area that appears to be related to intelligence is creativity.

Creativity

As the ability to produce valued outcomes in a novel way, creativity is a broad area. Creative people do not simply act in an original way; the outcome of their behaviour is appropriate and useful (Mumford and Gustafson, 1988). Intelligence, it seems, is required for creativity – having an IQ of 120 or above is usual in creative people – but high intelligence is no guarantee of creative thought. It is also very difficult to measure, but unlike intelligence not because we cannot define it, but because creativity is not uniform. One strategy is to examine *divergent thinking*. This involves finding unusual ways of solving problems, or generating multiple possibilities. Try thinking of all the possible uses of a brick. Conventional responses would be the more usual uses, such as building, etc. Unusual responses are thought to indicate creative thought, but may simply be measuring originality. The real measure of creativity is whether the solution or possibility is appropriate, but novel. Another strategy is to measure thought processes in creativity, or the personal characteristics of creative people (Wakefield, 1991). This would tend to suggest that creativity is as much a function of personality as it is of cognition. There is also evidence to suggest that creative people may be more predisposed towards mental disorder (Jamison, 1994).

Summary

Intelligence and creativity are two different types of outcome of thinking. Both have problems of definition and measurement. If intelligence is seen as the cognitive ability to respond and adapt to the environment, and develops either via a child's maturation or expansion of the knowledge base, then creativity is linked to it. Most creative people are intelligent, but not all intelligent people are creative.

Creativity is also linked to expertise, although experts are not always creative. A common notion is that experts are made, but creative geniuses are born – a return to the nature/nurture debate. The next chapter will look at the way in which expertise might develop, and how to measure it.

Self-test Questions

1 Why does the psychometric approach cause difficulties for Cognitive Psychological examination of intelligence?
2 What are the major differences between stage theories and the information processing approach to cognitive development?
3 Write down as many uses for a brick as you can.

CHAPTER 12

Learning, Skill and Expertise

Key terms

classical conditioning learning in which an environmental stimulus produces a response
cognitive map a mental representation
expertise a high level of skill, probably involving different types of pattern storage
knowledge engineering a specialised set of research methods designed to elicit knowledge from experts
latent learning learning that takes place without being immediately manifest in behaviour
operant conditioning learning in which positive reinforcement of a behaviour increases the probability of that behaviour being produced, or negative reinforcement decreases the probability
reinforcer an environmental consequence of behaviour
skill an ability to use specialised behaviour – motor, social or cognitive – to complete tasks

Key names

Bandura • Fitts and Posner • Johnson-Laird • Pavlov • Rotter • Seligman • Skinner • Tolman

In any study of cognition, we need to examine how people use the information they acquire, not only in the everyday ways of decision making and problem solving, but also in the use of skill and expert knowledge. This chapter will demonstrate how we might apply the findings of Cognitive Psychology to examine how an expert in a particular field works. To set the scene for such an examination, let us first find out a little more about how we learn.

Learning

Traditional studies of learning concentrated on conditioning, classical and operant.

Classical Conditioning

Classical conditioning was first examined by Pavlov (1927). Pavlov's work is that which has given us the procedures and the terminology. He was working on the digestive system of the dog, and accidentally found that dogs will produce saliva when shown food *and* when the dogs saw the technician that usually fed them. This salivating can also be produced in response to an arbitrary signal (say, a bell) which has become associated with the giving of food. The Pavlovian terminology that developed from these experiments is given below.

- Food is the unconditioned stimulus (US) as it invariably (unconditionally) produces the saliva.
- The salivation is the unconditioned response (UR) because it needs no artificial connection with the US to be produced.
- The bell is a conditioned stimulus (CS) because it has the ability to produce the response.
- Salivation response to the CS alone is now a conditioned response (CR).
- When the CR occurs in response to the CS, this is known as a conditioned reflex, *reinforced* by the US.

The learning which takes place under these circumstances is now known as classical or Pavlovian conditioning.

Operant Conditioning

We have already discussed Thorndike's experiments with cats, and their accidental learning about how to escape from boxes. This showed an alternative to the Pavlovian idea of learning, and was refined and extended by Skinner (1938). The conditioning in this case, being an accidental form of learning, was called instrumental or operant conditioning. Skinner used rats and pigeons in his experiments. They were conditioned to press or peck a bar in a contraption now known as a 'Skinner box' in return for food.

Some of the terms, but not all, are interchangeable between the two types of conditioning. Food is still called a reinforcer in operant conditioning, and when the responses decline on removal of the reward, this is known as extinction.

So we have a picture of learning being the acquisition of new responses, or the formation of associations between stimulus and response. This forms the basis of the behaviourist approach. Classical conditioning means an individual will learn a new signal, and operant conditioning means learning the relationship between behaviour and outcomes (Rescorla, 1992). However, not all learning can be accounted for in this way. Outside the limited experimental paradigms in which Pavlov and Skinner studied conditioning and learning, the story is a little more complex. For example, it is very easy to make the learned response disappear if unpleasant stimuli are applied (Mackintosh, 1983). The other difficulty with looking at these studies, carried out on animals, is that the more complex learning seen in humans is not explained by these simple models. If we turn to cognitive theories of learning, we see attempts to explain and explore learning outside the behaviourist approach.

Learning and Cognitive Processes

The behaviourist theory of learning fails to account for much of human learning because it ignores the contribution of cognitive processes, or mental activity. The cognitive approach emphasises the role of understanding, but does not reject the role of conditioning. Rather it proposes that learners are information seekers, wishing to make sense of relationships between items and events. This approach to learning emphasises the cognition of the individual, and the social environment in which learning takes place.

The cognitive–social theory of learning proposes that cognitive processes mediate between the environmental stimuli and the individual's behaviour, and that therefore learning is socialised. An early study that supports this idea is that of Tolman (1948), who demonstrated that rats develop mental representations of mazes that they learn. These *cognitive maps*, according to Tolman, are responsible for *latent learning*. Tolman had three groups of rats. Each attempted to learn the maze, but one group was always given food on successful completion. This group learnt the maze quickly, and became error-free very quickly too. The second group was never rewarded, and did not learn the maze, never becoming error-free. The third group were also denied food, for ten trials, and were not successful in completing the maze quickly or without errors, until the food started appearing. At this point, group three quickly reached the same level of success as the group that had been rewarded consistently. The argument here is that the rate at which group three caught up with group one must mean that they had learnt the maze, but the absence of the reward was mediating their behaviour. They had a mental representation or cognitive map, or they would have had to go through the same rate of progress as group one had, but the demonstration of their having learnt the maze was too quick for this.

The cognitive theory of learning also proposes that *expectancy* predicts the likelihood of behaviour occurring (Rotter, 1954). Expectation of outcome or consequences of behaviour will determine whether we do something or not. There are several items that contribute to this:

► *Locus of control* refers to the general type of expectancy we hold about the outcomes of our behaviour (Rotter, 1990). Having an internal locus of control means the individual will believe he or she can control his or her fate, whereas an external locus leads people to believe their lives are determined by forces outside themselves. Learning how to behave in certain situations means we learn to anticipate the links between action and outcome, and the locus of control we have determines how likely we are to learn this anticipation.

► *Learned helplessness* is the belief that we cannot escape from aversive stimuli, and the problems associated with this idea. Seligman (1975) gave dogs electric shocks from which they could not escape. When they had learnt that escape was impossible, they gave up, and exhibited signs very much akin to human depression. Learned helplessness is the expectancy of non-escape.

► *Explanatory style* is the individual way in which we perceive events, particularly unfavourable ones. A pessimistic explanatory style perceives bad events as stable and global, and impossible to change. Peterson and Seligman (1984) suggested that differential responses to the situation that can lead to learned helplessness account for the different ways in which they respond.

In addition to the above, psychologists also agree that observation plays a large part in learning. We learn by observing others, and how they behave, and what happens to them if they behave in a particular way (Bandura, 1967). *Tutelage* or direct instruction is also involved here.

We cannot only learn from what we are told and what we observe, but also gain advice, which turns into plans. Trying out plans, and experiencing them fail, is also an aid to learning. But learning can also work by generalising from facts and refining (specialising) these generalisations via further facts. This is known as induction.

So, we have several possible theories for the way in which we learn. It is likely that some simple elements are learnt by the simple stimulus–response linkage, but that complex learning is a combination of environmental experience, social observation and cognitive mediation. We now need to examine what we learn. Much of Cognitive Psychology is concerned with the acquisition of skills, how we learn to use language, how we solve problems and make decisions, etc. There are several types of skill. Motor skills are those involving physical and computational effort; social skills are those which make the individual socially competent. Cognitive skills are characterised as performance on tasks where motor responses are relatively simple, but which require higher-order cognitive processes. We will concentrate on cognitive skills.

Cognitive Skills

The acquisition of cognitive skills has been studied extensively in the laboratory. In 1967, Fitts and Posner proposed a model that involves three stages:

1 *Early or cognitive stage*: Understanding of task, and application of attention to requisite information.
2 *Intermediate or associative stage*: Attempts to use strategies allowing rapid perception and retrieval of information and response. Elimination of errors and increase in performance speed.
3 *Late or autonomous stage*: Correct responses become automatic, error-free performance and speed increases.

This model has been tested in the laboratory, and an example of one such study will demonstrate how the stages work.

Participants learned to give true or false responses to a task where they must identify whether a given letter is *n* letters after another in the alphabet (Table 12.1). Initially, participants were slow, as they were accessing the following letters before responding; the greater the sequence number they had to count through, the longer the response time. With practice, they left this early stage and became quicker and more accurate at counting (associative). With more practice, they were able to use past experience to directly access the patterns, and response time became independent of the number of letters they had to count through, as indeed they were no longer counting but using patterns (Compton and Logan, 1991).

This three-stage model is applicable to the acquisition of cognitive skills in everyday life. For example, watch children who are learning to manipulate numbers and you will see them counting on their fingers, but eventually they progress to internalising the counting and familiarity with single-digit additions. Multiplication is finally achieved as retrieval from the dreaded 'times tables'. Skill acquisition does not always follow the three-stage model, however; handwriting does not necessarily improve with practice and time. The advent of word-processing has probably made this even more true, and the addition of spell-checking has probably made typing less accurate However, having learnt one word-processing package, the transfer of this skill to another package becomes easier.

Table 12.1 *Three-stage model test*

Question	Letters	Answer
Is B + 3 = E?	B C D E	True
Is N + 3 = R?	N O P Q	False
Is H + 2 + J?	H I J	True

> domain a particular field of
> expertise or knowledge

When we learn information in a particular *domain* we are attempting to become experts. Expertise is the highest level of cognitive skill, and an important area in Cognitive Psychology.

Expertise

The major questions in the acquisition and use of expert knowledge are concerned with the storing, organisation and use of information, just the same problems that Cognitive Psychology attempts to address. There are various ways of viewing expertise. To the uninitiated, expert knowledge is mysterious, acquired through years of experience and requiring superior intellect. From 'outside' expertise seems to be based on intuition, together with application of logic beyond the non-expert. Cognitive Psychology offers rather more subtle and objective definitions. Expertise is based on large banks of specific and organised knowledge. Experts know if a problem is within the scope of their knowledge, or if rules need to be used from related domains.

A major approach to studying expertise has been to look at the difference between novices and experts. Often a cognitive science approach has been used involving traditional research methods and protocol analysis, a qualitative method criticised for its dependence on interpretation and high level of ambiguity (Patel and Groen, 1986). However, there is a well-established precedent for using this to provide data for cognitive modelling (see Johnson-Laird, 1983; Slack, 1984).

Novice to Expert

Novices and experts differ significantly in their use of knowledge and their performance of the skill. Examining these differences can give insight into how knowledge changes and is used. Using a mixture of laboratory and real-life observations, the distinctions (manifest in items such as memory and performance) between the two groups can be determined. These distinctions, according to Rumelhart and Norman (1978), take three forms:

1 Accretion – the accumulation of new knowledge into existing cognitive structures.
2 Tuning – adaptations to existing structures as a result of changes in knowledge.
3 Restructuring – major changes in structures due to inefficiencies dealing with knowledge.

Such changes reflect the types of structure in knowledge itself. That further organisation takes place in knowledge is clear. The fuzzy and hierarchical nature of knowledge would appear to be generic to all domains, and the greater the complexity of a task within a domain, the more organisation is needed in the knowledge. In addition to inherent organisation, the activation of pattern recognition also takes place in expert performance (Chase and Ericsson, 1982). Such organisation is evident in, for example, musical performance (Krumhansl, 1990; Lim and Lippman, 1991). Together with shifts from declarative to procedural knowledge structures, many domains must incorporate elements of physical practice in order to achieve expertise. To quote Luciano Pavarotti: 'Learning music by reading about it, is like making love by mail'.

All of the speculation above about expert knowledge is supported when expert performance is examined. The retained knowledge is not subject to interference on recall (Reder and Ross, 1983). Performance also appears automated, i.e. not dependent on memory limitations, runs to completion, requires practice to speed, and is unavailable to introspection. Experts also change strategies when required (Weilinga and Breuker, 1986). Such elements are applicable in our example of music. Adaptations take place in the transition from novice musician to expert. What parent of a prospective violinist has not been amazed (and relieved) when the pupil achieves, at long last, the skill of intonation? This is, quite simply, tuning, to tuning. Even the musician who claims ignorance of musical theory is in possession of facts about music. Musical performance also demonstrates the same generic elements as in other domains, for example pattern recognition can be seen quite clearly in sight reading and the associated 'chunking errors' (Sloboda, 1991; Halpern and Bower, 1982). It appears, too, to be subject to the same limitations and organisation as other domains. Such assertions, then, lead us to be more likely to accept the statement of Sloboda *et al.* (1994b) that it is practice that makes perfect, not inherited genius.

It appears then that there are two types of knowledge acquired while becoming an expert: facts and rules. The organisation of these is of paramount importance. It is estimated that in order to acquire different types of knowledge, an individual must learn between 300 (for an 'A' level subject) and 1 million (for a medical degree) facts (Larkin *et al.*, 1988). But facts by themselves, in a passive form, are useless. Rules are needed, particularly production rules (see Chapter 9): an expert needs a minimum of 10,000 rules (Hayes-Roth, 1985). Expert knowledge appears to be stored and used in a variety of ways.

The Storage and Use of Expert Knowledge

It is likely that expert knowledge is stored in the categorical structures we have already discussed in Chapter 9, but that the discrimination between and within categories is finer. For example, a non-expert might simply identify a creature as a 'bird', but an ornithologist would discriminate size, colour, height, and many more attributes. Concept boundaries may become blurred, as many attributes will become associated with other categories. So expert knowledge is 'fuzzy' in nature – configurations of attributes become the norm for storage, and organisation becomes qualitatively different. In addition to the naive representation of a novice, experts may have a second model overlaying the first. Expertise is also related to the speed of access, and perceptual patterns could be efficiently indexed. Chase and Simon (1973), for example, report the ability of chess players to recognise configurations of pieces on the board, whereas novices are still examining the relationship between placement and moves. There is a similar effect in other domains (Chase and Ericsson, 1982). This indexing would therefore mean that experts do not have to search through a large number of possibilities to find a solution. There is also evidence of higher use of procedural knowledge, with a stage where the knowledge is 'compiled' and hence strengthened and tuned, which makes for more difficult reflection on the use of knowledge.

If the knowledge becomes stored efficiently, and it is difficult to make explicit what it is, then perhaps examining its use would be more informative. Experts show greater and more efficient recall of domain-specific knowledge despite having a great many facts to search, and they are not subject to interference in the retrieval (see Chapter 8). So there is an integration of associated facts, more effective encoding and the use of inference. A great deal of expert skill becomes automated too, in comparison with the use of the skill by novices, and the navigation of the knowledge is more efficient. Evidence suggests that experts use different strategies for reasoning with the knowledge (Anderson, 1983). Novices use a means–end analysis. Larkin (1981) looked at the domain of physics and suggested that when novices attempt to find the velocity of an object, they start with this unknown property. An expert, though, knows that acceleration needs to be found first, and possibly other quantities too, and therefore proceeds *towards* the velocity property. This is known as forward chaining, and uses significantly fewer cognitive resources than the backward chaining of the novice. Diagnostic medicine, on the other hand, uses a combination of reasoning strategies. Due to uncertainty, a diagnosis may need to be confirmed with tests. Certain patterns of symptoms may suggest various illnesses (forward inference) but may be imperfectly associated with a specific category and hence require the sub-diagnoses to be eliminated (backward chaining). So an expert must know what strategy to use.

All of the above means that expertise relies heavily on large banks of domain-specific facts negotiated using rules. These are organised into associated patterns that allow for better retrieval. This retrieved knowledge can be used in a variety of ways depending on the area of expertise and the requirements of the situation. The difficulty we have as psychologists is that the knowledge the expert has acquired has become so embedded in automatic processes, and so proceduralised, that it is not available to verbalisation. So how can we study it? If the experts themselves cannot comment on the expertise, we have no way of knowing what we are trying to examine.

Also, the practice of the expertise is often not possible to examine in the laboratory; it must be carried out in the field. The next section will look at ways in which expertise might be studied, and the more specialised methods of Cognitive Psychology/Cognitive Science.

Studying Expertise

Laboratory techniques necessarily must break down and isolate pieces of behaviour in order to examine them. This might not be feasible for expertise. One approach allied to cognitive science is knowledge engineering. This set of techniques was developed in the building of expert systems. Knowledge engineering covers the elicitation of knowledge from experts, knowledge representation, and system development. There are three general method-ologies employed in knowledge elicitation:

1 Interviews and subsequent analysis of verbal data.
2 Observation and running commentary.
3 Personal constructs.

Interviews

The objective of interviews is to gain complete and accurate descriptions of the expert's knowledge and how it is handled. *Critical incident* interviews ask the expert to describe cases which have, for some reason, stuck in his or her mind. Difficult or interesting cases are more memorable, but may be atypical. Once they are examined, the researcher will use these to examine how the processes described might be used in more generalised situations. This might be followed up with *reclassification* interviews. Given the goal (decision) the expert can specify what evidence would be used to make a decision, and working backwards intermediate decisions can be examined.

Another form of interview used might be those based on conversation theory (Pask, 1975). This is not what we mean by everyday conversation; it looks at concepts made public by talking about them. Johnson and Johnson (1988) used this effectively in *teachback* interviews, where the expert tells the researcher how to do a particular task, then the researcher 'teaches' the expert back, until the expert is satisfied the researcher knows about the task. Johnson and Johnson suggest the strength of this technique is that both global and specific structure from the domain can be accessed, and authenticated during the analysis. The problem here is that the researcher is actually becoming an expert too, and obviously this is not suitable for every domain.

Observation

A useful technique in any field, direct observation is excellent where the researcher can remain in the background and the expert talks through what is happening. There are obviously many domains where this would not be possible, such as confidential medical diagnosis. However, where it is possible, then subsequent reference can be used with the expert examining thoughts and behaviour retrospectively. To reduce errors of interpretation, events can be taped (video or audio) and material extracted and refined into relationships and rules, often called *protocols*.

Personal Constructs

Personal construct theory was first explored by Kelly (1955). Whilst it is not appropriate to expand on the theory here, what we can examine is how it might be applied to the study of knowledge. According to Kelly, each person is a personal scientist, seeking to predict and control events by formulating hypotheses about the world. A personal construct is a conceptual framework used to analyse differences and similarities in the environment experienced. Knowledge bases can be generated from the examination of an individual's personal constructs, and from an amalgamation of constructs from a group. For a more detailed description of how personal constructs can be used to elicit knowledge, and the way in which novices change to experts, the reader is directed to Shaw (1981) and Gavin (1992).

Summary

The examination of cognitive processes in isolation is often not useful or educational. If we look at a particular area such as expert knowledge, and the way that experts acquire, store, organise and use their knowledge, then some of the issues with which Cognitive Psychology is concerned become clear. In this chapter we have looked at several theories of how we might learn, and what that means for expertise. In the next chapters we will explore another area that has several aspects of learning, comprehension and use of knowledge – language.

Self-test Questions

1 What are the differences and similarities between classical and operant conditioning?
2 Why does the behavioural approach to learning not offer a full explanation?
3 What can the cognitive approach tell us about learning?
4 How might skills be acquired?
5 What differentiates experts from novices?

CHAPTER 13

Language Acquisition and Development

Key terms

critical periods biologically determined stages of organic and cognitive development during which language must be acquired

language acquisition the way in which we learn to use language. There are three major theories – the behaviourist, the innate and the information processing views

language acquisition device pre-programmed 'wiring' in the brain required for learning to use language in response to environmental stimuli

language development the way in which the use of language can be observed to change and the underlying skill development this implies

morphemes the smallest meaning units of language

phonemes the smallest sound units of language

transformational grammar the rules by which sentences are transformed into meaning, and meaning into sentences

Key names

Aitchison • Bates • Chomsky • Lenneberg • Morgan • Piaget

Just about every human being learns to talk, or use language in some way. This is a tremendous achievement. Babies come into the world without language, although every parent would say that the baby can communicate its needs very well. By about a year old, the first words are being spoken, and a little later sentences are heard from their mouths. During the first years of schooling and growing a child learns to use language in the same way that adults do. How does this happen?

Language Acquisition – the Behaviourist View

Behaviourist tradition would have it that a child learns by imitation. Observation of the world, and the language that communicates about it, leads children to acquire the use of speech (Skinner, 1957). But language is very

127

complex. If we imitated what we heard, we would only use the words and sentences we hear. The number of unique combinations of words is huge, so we cannot be learning by imitation alone. Also, children make errors in language they will not have heard from adults. The creativity and fallibility in language rules out the behaviourist view as a complete explanation.

Language Acquisition – the Innate View

Children are expert learners of language, much better than adults. If you try to learn a second language, you will agree with that assertion. It appears that there are innate learning abilities, especially for linguistic, and this applies to any language. Children learn the language that is spoken to them, but have the capability to learn any. A child born in England, but hearing another language, will learn that one, so the learning ability is not culturally bound.

Due to the fact that all humans seem to be able to learn language, psycholinguists think that children have innate programming to learn. Chomsky (1959) argued that there are specific skills enabling us to learn, and was opposed to the behaviourist ideas of language acquisition. The latter used the model of operant conditioning put forward by Skinner, which proposed that language was learnt via reinforcement, with parents shaping utterances from children by approval. The creativity and flexibility of language rules out this explanation according to Chomsky. He argued that children develop hypotheses about the rules of the language to which they are exposed, and that these hypotheses are initially generated due to the innate abilities. The use of the hypotheses is governed by parameters, depending on the language (Chomsky, 1986). Experimental evidence for this is difficult to envisage, but naturalistic research does suggest some support. For example, parents tend to talk to children with a limited set of words and phrases, which are short and grammatically correct (Harris and Coltheart, 1986). This simple language, it is thought, might provide children with an easily analysed internal lexicon on which to test hypotheses.

So we can see that the question of how children acquire language is a difficult one, with testable evidence difficult to come by. It is also closely linked to the child's understanding of the words heard. There is a gap between understanding and production, which suggests a deeper cognitive ability than mere imitation (Bates *et al.*, 1988). But children will also use words that they clearly do not understand. Bates *et al.* suggested that there were two lines of lexical development, one centred on comprehension, and the other fixed on words that are learnt by rote. All this indicates the complexity of language acquisition.

In addition to the complex set of processes used, there also appear to be critical periods for acquiring language. These are biologically predetermined, and if a child has not learnt particular parts of language by the time the critical period has passed, then he or she never will (Lenneberg, 1967). It has long been established that there are also language areas of the brain that develop in the first two years of life, and this development is associated with the rapid learning of new words. For example, at about the time they start school, children are learning up to 20 new words a day (Goldman-Rakic, 1987). Try doing that now in a second language, or even your own!

> phonemes are the smallest functional acoustic units. They are not necessarily directly associated with letters or syllables. The word 'rat' has three phonemes, 'r', 'a' and 't', but so does mouse: 'm', 'ow' and 'ss'
>
> morphemes are the smallest functional units of meaning. They are not necessarily directly associated with words. The word 'rat' is a morpheme, but the word 'rats' has two morphemes, the meaning of 'rat', and the suffix 's' which pluralises it

Chomsky takes all this as indicative of an innate ability to acquire a language. He suggests that our brains are born with 'hard wiring' ready for developing language areas, and acquiring language. He calls this wiring a *language acquisition device* or LAD (Chomsky, 1972), which is something we have when born, but which needs the appropriate social environment to develop properly. Further support for this idea of 'innateness' is that parts of language are similar, no matter what language it is. There are a limited number of *phonemes* in human speech, but a much greater variety of sounds that can be made. English contains about 40. If we put together all the phonemes of known languages, we only get some of the sounds that human speech contains. In every language phonemes and *morphemes* form the larger units via a hierarchical structure. Also, all languages are fully developed, and can express all the ideas that the cultural group needs to communicate. Just because a language does not express the concepts of higher-order philosophical analysis it does not mean that the language or the cultural group to which it belongs is cognitively underdeveloped or primitive; it is simply that they may have more important things to talk about.

So observing the world of language leads psycholinguists to propose this 'innateness' view. It focuses on the structure of language, and how we process and understand it.

> transformational grammar an attempt to explain how people convert between surface structure and deep structure. Rules are followed in order to translate any sentence structure into something directly meaningful

There are two levels of structure. Surface structure refers to words and their place in the sentence, and deep structure refers to the underlying meaning of language. Rules that relate the two structures are concerned with *transformational grammar* (Chomsky, 1957).

The innate approach to language aims to develop understanding of such grammars, and how we use language so flexibly. This will be examined in more detail in the next chapter.

Language Acquisition – the Information Processing View

Arguments against the behaviourist view say that it does not account for the creativity in language. Arguments against the innateness view say that there is still no explanation of how language is acquired, and how we go about monitoring our use of language. The innate viewpoint is basically one of linguistics rather than psychology, and while we do not reject it because of that, it still does not address some fundamental questions.

The information processing approach looks at the mental abilities involved in language, and how they are linked to other capacities. The Piagetian approach to cognitive development is very influential here (Piaget, 1959). Piaget was concerned with how children develop through several distinct but linked stages towards adult thought, and hence use of language. Knowledge of language is insufficient for its appropriate use; the child must also have developed the concepts that accompany it. The information processing approach places more emphasis on the environmental input a child experiences, which will facilitate the acquisition of knowledge and language. Accompanying this is the maturation of the brain (Morgan, 1990).

Each of the above viewpoints has something to its merit. It is unlikely that one will provide a full explanation for language acquisition, and more probable that a combination of them is the true view.

Having examined the ways in which language can be acquired, the next point to investigate is how it develops. This is a little easier to think about, as the stages that a child goes through are easily observed.

Stages of Language Development

There are several factors which appear to be important for language learning. Babies are very social creatures, and find humans a very interesting part of their environment. They will follow movements of the people around them with their eyes as soon as they can focus on them, and attract attention by various sounds. Children raised without human contact (so-called *feral* children) have an impoverished language environment, and demonstrate a lack of language development that can be put down to having had no response to early sounds they make. So the first factor that is important for language development is social interaction. Also, babies are born able to make sounds, they have all the apparatus they need (ask any parent of a new baby), and appear to try out all the sounds during babbling (see below). It even appears that babies can distinguish particular sounds in the womb, and show preferences for firstly the mother's voice (well, it is the one they hear the most before they are born) and even particular stories.

Children between one and four months can distinguish between phonemes. If a baby is played a certain sound, and has to suck in order to hear the sound, the sucking rate will increase, until the baby habituates to that phoneme. When the sucking rate has decreased to one sound, playing a different one will make the sucking rate increase again.

So, children do have a predisposition to learning language. There are several clear stages to the development of language. These stages are not necessarily distinct, neither is there necessarily a smooth passage from one to the other. The ages are also simply a guideline; a lot of parental worry has been generated by child-rearing books that suggest that if baby isn't using words by a year old there is something wrong. Stages can be affected by many things, such as very rapid development of other cognitive or motor skills, which might take up a lot of maturing, or even something as simple as birth order. Many parents have observed that the second or third child seems slower in using words than the older children, and this could be that the older children are speaking for their younger siblings.

Table 13.1 shows the stages of language development, and the approximate ages of the child when the activity is seen. It also shows what other skills are developing at the same time.

These stages of language, intellectual and motor development are all clearly observable, or testable. When a baby is new-born the cries heard are all the same, but eventually they begin to be differentiated. Parents will learn to identify which cries mean the baby is hungry, upset, etc., and these appear to have universality. Crying, though, is purely reflexive, and not the attempt to communicate, but they are certainly developing their lungs! An infant's cries are at a pitch which it is difficult to ignore, and there appears to be an in-built response to them, even when we are not the parent of the baby. Try living next door to a house where there is a new baby (and thin walls) and seeing if *you* can stay asleep!

Cooing is a vowel-like sound, but without true acoustic properties. Again the function of cooing appears to be to elicit responses (adults will invariably coo back at a baby) and to develop the vocal cords. The addition of consonants to the cooing is another form of playing with sound, which is called babbling. Unfortunately for doting parents, baby is *not* saying 'dada' or 'mama' but experimenting with chains of sound. Babbling, unlike crying and cooing, is not universal, but is very common, and is influenced by the language heard. It is possible to identify the nationality of a babbling baby simply by listening to tapes. This is known as *babbling drift,* the idea that during this phase, children learn to restrict the sounds produced to those contained in the language around them, and use the intonation patterns (rise and fall of speech sounds). Babbling can often sound like real speech if you don't listen too hard.

Whether a child babbles or not, the first words appear at about 12 months. The child uses one word to communicate a whole idea; often this stage is therefore called the *holophrastic stage.* The meaning of the child's utterance has to be decided by the context in which it is said, and this is often very successful. A child may say 'shoe', but depending on the context it could be 'I want to put my shoes on' or 'I want to take my shoes off' or 'where are my shoes?'. It is some achievement to select one word which is going to communicate an idea to the carer. The problem here is that the use

Table 13.1 *Development of language and accompanying skills*

Age	Language stage	Other accompanying skills being developed
Birth	Crying	
6 weeks	Cooing	
6 months	Babbling (introduction of consonant sounds)	Sitting with support, reaching
8 months	Intonation added	
1 year	One-word utterances, some understanding	Standing, walking with support
18 months	Two-word utterances, repertoire of up to 50 words, more understanding	Unaided walking, attempts stairs (backwards!) The child is still exploring the world through sensations and actions
2 years	Word inflections. Observed wish to communicate	Running, but poor balance. Attempts stairs (one foot leading) Object permanence (child understands that objects do not disappear if hidden)
2.5 years	Questions and negatives	Jumping and standing on one foot Better balance, which is transferred to construction with toys
5 years	Complex constructions, large vocabulary, grammar close to adult	Tiptoeing, climbs or descends stairs with alternate feet, good balance. Symbolic thought develops, as does object permanence, some egocentrism remains
10 years	Mature speech	Good mental representation, concept of conservation is developed (basic properties of objects remain stable, even though superficial properties may be changed, such as pouring 1 litre of water from a beaker of one shape to another)
12+ years	Vocabulary develops in respect of conceptual development	Application of logic, hypothetical thinking

vocabulary is limited, probably owing to lack of conceptual experience, and children overextend the use of a word. Many male parents become upset when every man is referred to as 'daddy', but it is simply because the child is generalising, much the same way as they might say 'moon' to refer to any round shiny object. Under-extensions also occur.

Later, two-word utterances are used, with an accompanying increase in vocabulary. The *mean length of utterances* (MLU) increases too; this is the number of morphemes the child is using. The appropriate use of syntax appears, although some contextual analysis must be done to understand what the child means (Bloom, 1970). This stage is referred to as *telegraphic speech* because two-word usage sounds like the child is being economical with utterance. Here we might hear 'Mummy shoe' which translates as the child wanting the mother to help with putting on shoes.

As the number of words in a chain increases to three- or four-word utterances, the child begins to learn word order and use inflection. Inflection means the form of the word depending on its meaning. English is a poor example of this; our language tends to rely very much on word order. Anyone who has learnt Latin, however, will realise that the endings of words mean that they can appear in various orders; it is the form of the words that give the intent.

Syntax is mostly mastered by the age of 5–6 years, but some interpretation of sentences is still difficult, owing to incomplete understanding of the different meanings of words (Aitchison, 1983). Full maturity of speech is not reached until the age of about 10, when other intellectual capabilities are becoming fully formed too.

Summary

Having explored the theories of how language is acquired, and the stages we go through in developing this skill, we need to examine how we learn to process and understand language. However, it would be prudent to first look at the structure of language. The next chapter will therefore do just that, before discussing how we use language.

Self-test Questions

1 What evidence is there to suggest the existence of a language acquisition device?
2 At what point is a child explicitly trying to communicate?
3 Why is crying said to be a reflexive response rather than true communication?

CHAPTER 14

Structure and Comprehension of Language

Key terms

aphasia difficulties with spoken language after brain damage
deep structure the underlying meaning of sentences
dyslexia difficulties with written language, either developmental or acquired
parsing the process of syntactic analysis
pragmatics the intention of language
semantics the meaning of words
surface structure the order of words in sentences
syntax the structure of language

Key names

Allport • Brown and Yule • Chomsky • Critchley • Grice • Miller • Sperber and
   Wilson

We are such expert users of our own language that it is easy to forget how
complex it is. We can recognise thousands of words, and their meaning, and
we know how to construct these into sentences. We also know whether or not
a sentence is grammatically acceptable. This chapter is devoted to a discussion of language structure and use.

   Language has three basic components: syntax, semantics and pragmatics.

Language Structure

Syntax – Relation of Signs to Each Other

We normally speak in constructions such as sentences. What is, and is not, an
appropriate structure for constructions is the syntax of a language.

   It has been argued that the sentence is an artificial unit created by the
advent of writing. Written text is a fairly recent development, and there are

still cultures which do not rely on it. Even in 'literate' cultures, speech often does not entirely consist of complete sentences (Brown and Yule, 1983). Analysis of speech, in which we use pauses and fillers (such as 'er', 'you know' and so on), suggests that the real unit of language is the clause. We tend to use the fillers just before clauses, er which are parts of sentences which can, you know, stand alone.

However, whatever level of construction we use must be understandable, and there are rules which everyone uses, albeit unconsciously.

The major development in psychological studies of syntax started with Chomsky in 1957. He looked at the syntactic analysis of sentences, suggesting that syntax rules were used to generate meaningful constructions. For example, look at the sentence 'the cat scratched the dog'. Chomsky said that this sentence could be represented by a tree structure as illustrated in Figure 14.1. The sentence (S) is composed of a noun phrase (NP) and a verb phrase (VP). The NP has an article (art) and a noun (N), and the VP is further broken down into a verb (V) and another noun phrase. This syntactic analysis is called *parsing*, and is the application of phrase structure rules.

There are a limited number of these phrase structure rules, but a huge number of sentences can be constructed using them. Sentences with very different structures can have the same meaning. Chomsky was interested in this, and drew a distinction between surface and deep structure. Surface structure relates to word order, whereas deep structure refers to the grammatical generation of the sentence. So 'the cat scratched the dog' and 'the dog was scratched by the cat' have the same deep structure, but very different surface structure. The first form is in the active voice, whereas the second is passive. In Chomsky's theory the phrase structure rules generate the deep structure, and transformational rules map the deep to the surface

Figure 14.1 *Parsing into syntax tree structure*

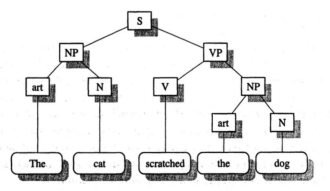

structure, which is actually spoken. What is spoken does not always fit with idealised rules of grammar, but people are good at recognising whether sentences are acceptable or not.

Thus Chomsky's 'transformational grammar' is an abstract description of language structure. The study of whether such linguistic rules relate to the psychological processes used in language is called *psycholinguistics*. Miller and McKean (1964) investigated the time taken to carry out transformations such as that between the two sentences above, from active to passive. They also looked at transformation between negative ('the cat did not scratch the dog') and positive. Using the time between being asked to transform the sentence and participants pressing a button to indicate they were ready to search through a list of alternative sentences to find the new form, they found that negative transformations were quickest, with passive transformations next, and passive+negative transformations longest:

passive	0.4 seconds
negative	0.9 seconds
passive + negative	1.5 seconds

This led them to conclude that transformations are performed sequentially, as single operations. However, this study was criticised as participants were constructing the transformations themselves, and there is no indication that this is how the natural process is carried out. There is also evidence to suggest that context of transformations is important (Wason, 1965; Slobin, 1966) and that it takes longer, for example, to verify implausible transformations, such as 'the dog ate the meat' to 'the meat ate the dog'. In other words, syntax is inextricably bound up with meaning. When we have something to say, we do not start with the structure of the sentences and then say it, we start with the meaning we wish to convey.

Semantics – Relation of Signs to Objects

Semantics is the study of the meaning of words alone and in longer constructions. If words are meaningless, then the object of language is lost. Communication, by either speaking or writing, is central to cognitive functioning, so it is very important for us to study semantics. Sperber and Wilson (1986) proposed the code model of verbal communication, in which thoughts are translated into words by a linguistic coding device for transmission, and when received by the listener (or reader) the linguistic coding device decodes them into appropriate meanings and thoughts. This is probably inadequate as a full explanation of combination.

The studies in semantic memory provide a different perspective on the use of words. Chapters 7 and 9 explored this in some detail. The psycholinguistic approach took such evidence and proposed several theories of how meaning is represented.

Feature theories suggest that meanings are stored in the mental lexicon in terms of shared features. However, this is only reasonable when looking at concrete nouns. Abstract words, adjectives, etc. are difficult to represent in this way, and are not always represented by one set of features.

Procedural semantics (Miller and Johnson-Laird, 1976) uses a computer simulation to examine representation of meaning. Using the feature theory as a basis, procedural operations can also be incorporated. In this way words other than concrete nouns can be added.

Pragmatics – Relation of Signs to Interpreters

The third area of linguistics is pragmatics. This is the study of why people choose to use the language in the particular way they do. Semantics is what words and sentences mean, whereas pragmatics is what users mean when speaking or writing. For example, the sentence 'I am now over here' can mean that the speaker wishes to impart some information, or can be an indirect request to join him or her. The major question is: how does the person being addressed identify the intended meaning? Studies in pragmatics suggested that there are three things extracted from utterances – reference, speech actions and implicatures (what is implied). These are analysed in terms of shared perceptual experience, previous conversations and shared culture. So if your friend mentions 'the man in the red car', he or she is assuming that you will identify this man as the most salient man in a red car in your current common experience. Reference is used and subsequently extracted in many ways. Demonstrative reference is accompanied by perhaps pointing when saying 'this is my friend with the red car'. Anaphoric reference refers to something mentioned earlier: 'my friend with the red car drove it round the block, then put it away in the garage'. The 'it' here is being used anaphorically.

Language use is active, involving utterance, illocutionary and perlocutionary acts. Utterance acts are the action of speaking, perlocutionary acts are the intent of the utterance. For example, if you asked your friend 'where is your car?' the utterance act is the act of speaking, the perlocutionary act is trying to get your friend to tell you where his car is now. The illocutionary act here is directive, the attempt to get the addressee to do something. Other illocutionary acts include assertives (expressions of belief), commissives (promises and offers), expressives (thanking, apologising, congratulating or greeting) and declarations. The addressee not only must hear the utterance, but must understand the illocutionary content. We do this by deriving the implicatures, i.e. what is implied from the utterance, by interpreting it against current purpose or direction of the exchanges, and the assumption that the speaker is co-operative (Grice, 1975). In other words, the context of exchanges is discourse, and cannot be separated from the comprehension and context of language.

Language Use

Knowledge and Comprehension

The comprehension of language is the ability to respond appropriately to messages in natural language. However, there is also the act of acquiring new knowledge, and in conversation we may learn of things not in our own personal experience, and through text learn of things in the past and distance. Language comprehension, then, is inseparable from our knowledge banks, both in the use of language, and in the hearing/reading of it. The study of comprehension is important as a major aspect of cognitive functioning, and for artificial intelligence (see Chapter 17).

To understand utterances, the person hearing or reading them must relate the linguistic content to knowledge stored. Language use then is a highly complex cognitive process, involving both the knowledge of a language and the general knowledge of the world. There are quite clear stages in the linguistic processing that leads to comprehension. In stage 1, parsing gives the initial syntactic structures, possibly by the categorical information derived from each word. In stage 2 more lexical and semantic information is derived, while stage 3 is a mapping from the parsing result onto this lexical information. An unsuccessful mapping forces re-analysis (Friederici, 1995). In this way, the initial perception is built up into a cognitive representation.

We have seen that language comprehension is a perceptual, analytical and representational process. Its use, however, is directly related to the underlying knowledge. In Chapter 12, we looked at expertise, and how experts develop from novices. One distinguishing aspect of an expert, in addition to actions, is the use of language. Context will always differentiate role. For example, suppose you and I look at the sky, and see a cloud. We would think 'Oh, a cloud, I wonder if it will rain today?'. A meteorologist would look at the cloud and decide its type, estimate its size, direction and doubtless hundreds of other variables, and decide whether or not it will rain today. A glider pilot, on the other hand, would look at the cloud and think 'A mountain wave, rising air and good lift for flying today'. Context and knowledge determine the use of the concept of cloud. Models of language assume that it is the currency of thought, and indicate role and culture. Given that, there are still some fundamental processes of the *production* of language that are the same no matter how we use it.

Language Production

One way of examining production of speech is to look at speakers' fluency. More cognitively demanding situations produce more pauses in the flow of speech, but as familiarity with the situation increases, so does fluency. Goldman-Eisler (1968) suggested that this meant people use pauses to plan high-level speech. Butterworth (1975) found that speech hesitations coincide with units of ideas, the development of an idea is indicated by a pause, then the speaker becomes fluent again, until the next idea is to be constructed. This reflects the underlying structure of language, and supports Brown and Yule's (1983) assertion that the sentence is not necessarily the natural unit of spoken language.

When constructing speech, we must reconstruct words from memory. In Chapter 9 we came across the idea of an internal lexicon where words and meaning are stored. Ellis and Beattie (1986) suggest that there is also a speech output lexicon, which stores the spoken form of words. The well-known *tip of the tongue* (TOT) phenomenon is thought to be a failure of this lexicon. Features of the word which we are attempting to retrieve are available, and using strategies such as thinking of the initial letter, length of the word, etc. can help (Brown and McNeill, 1966).

Again, context and role are important in language production. It must activate the knowledge of the listener and implies co-operation between speaker and listener. There appear to be several conventions of *maxims* that are followed in conversations (Grice, 1975). The *maxim of quantity* is important, as too little or too much information is unhelpful. Returning to our glider pilot talking about clouds, it would be insufficient to say simply the cloud is a 'mountain wave' if the listener knows nothing about gliding. An explanation of the terminology is required, but not so much that the listener cannot process it. However, the speaker can assume that the listener knows what a cloud is. The *maxim of quality* means that the speaker must be both informative and truthful, and the *maxim of relation* means that he or she must only use relevant information. The final requirement we have as listeners is that the speaker must attempt to be clear, the *maxim of manner*. So all lecturers obviously follow these rules, don't they? You never hear a lecturer assuming you know about elements of his or her topic, and hence giving too little information (quantity), lecturers *never* use sarcasm (quality), will not go off at a tangent (relation) and all your lectures have been clear (manner). Haven't they?

As with many areas of cognitive function, the evidence for the processes taking place comes from both laboratory studies and examination of functional disorder. Language is no exception.

Language Disorders

There are two major classes of language disorder – difficulties with spoken language known as *aphasia,* and difficulties with written language known as *dyslexia.*

Aphasia

Aphasia means the complete or partial loss of spoken language after brain damage. The cognitive neuropsychological study of aphasia assumes we can learn about the processing of language in the intact brain from the impaired performance of those with aphasia. For example, non-verbal cognitive skills appear to be intact in some patients with aphasic impairments, which suggests that they are separate from language processing (Allport, 1983).

Aphasia is not one disorder but can be seen in different forms. In the same way as amnesiac patients (see Chapter 8), the study tends to be by case study.

Anomia refers to difficulty with word retrieval, for example when trying to name objects. This is further classified into problems with semantic representation, and problems of retrieval of the spoken form of the word from the internal lexicon. The first category shows itself in naming errors, but of fine discrimination, in that patients may call a 'robin' a 'sparrow'. The second category shows full comprehension of the words the patient is trying to retrieve (they may point to the correct word when written, for example) but they cannot produce it. We can often experience a mild form of this when we feel that a word is 'on the tip of the tongue'. Often patients with word retrieval failure are able to construct grammatically correct sentences, but some are unable to use grammar correctly. This latter is known as *aggrammatism.*

Speech perception may also be a problem, a kind of word deafness. Although able to hear sounds perfectly, the patient cannot perceive speech correctly. Speech output can remain intact, as can reading comprehension.

Aphasic conditions usually occur after injury to the left hemisphere (right-handed patients) but some occur after right hemisphere damage. This often shows in lack of emotional content in spoken language, and failure to understand verbal humour and metaphor. Burgess and Chiarello (1996) suggest that while similar mechanisms are used to understand both literal and figurative speech, such as jokes and metaphors, there are possible different representational components to the two, so that neurological damage causes problems in higher-level cognitive processes.

Such findings suggest that an intact right hemisphere is necessary for high-level verbal processing in conjunction with other cognitive functions, whereas the left hemisphere is involved in the more basic verbal processing functions (Howard and Hatfield, 1987).

Dyslexia

There are two major forms of dyslexia. *Developmental dyslexia* is due to problems with development and language acquisition. *Acquired dyslexia* means that the condition has appeared in adulthood after brain damage.

Developmental dyslexia has been shown to have possible genetic causes, and to be more prevalent in males (Critchley, 1970). There are also possible cortical anomalies associated with the condition. Developmental dyslexia is characterised by *strephosymbolia* which mean that symbols are twisted around. This can take the form of reading or writing the mirror image of letters (*b* instead of *d*) or the letters of a whole word being written in the wrong order. In addition to such difficulties (where there is no retardation) dyslexics may be weak in telling left from right, have problems with time or date and in learning multiplication tables, be slow in naming colours, and recalling disconnected sequences of items.

Miles (1989) suggests that despite dyslexia being a reading problem, it is actually a phonological difficulty, as the errors arise when the dyslexic has to name incoming stimuli. Support for this comes from differences between children at pre-reading ages, and it appears that dyslexics are late in acquiring oral language skills. Such findings led researchers to suppose that dyslexia is an impairment to the *input* to the internal lexicon. When items are stored already, they can be used efficiently (hence normal performance on intellectual tests), but it takes more time to encode new items. Further support for this comes from the possibility that dyslexia is less of a problem in some languages than in others. Where speech sounds have direct relation with written forms, such as Italian, or where sounds are represented pictorially such as Japanese, dyslexia seems less pronounced than in English, where often there is little relation between written and spoken form (Thomson, 1984).

For a more detailed discussion of developmental dyslexia have a look at Galaburda (1989).

Acquired dyslexia is of more interest to the neuropsychologist. There is no suggestion that developmental dyslexia is the result of brain damage, but it is an impairment of linguistic development. Brain-injured patients, on the other hand, can exhibit different levels of acquired language problems. The two major types are *peripheral dyslexia*, in which patients have difficulty with visual perception of letters, and *central dyslexia*, impairment in processing meaning of written words. As with aphasia, the condition shows itself after left hemisphere damage. The exception to this is a form of peripheral acquired dyslexia, known as *neglect dyslexia*, in which right hemisphere damage leads to patients failing to read the leftmost letters on each line, or replacing them with another letter.

For a more detailed discussion of acquired dyslexia have a look at Coltheart *et al.* (1987).

Summary

We have looked at how language is acquired, constructed and used, how it develops, and what difficulties with language might show us. Language is the output end of the cognitive system. Information is sensed and perceived, then encoded, stored and organised. This information is transformed to knowledge and used in thoughts. The representation of those thoughts is in language. In this way we have seen how the human cognitive system processes and uses information. The next thing to examine is information processes other than the human. What can we learn from other entities on this world?

Self-test Questions

1 Why might sentences not be the natural unit of spoken language?
2 What are the stages of language processing?
3 What differentiates the TOT phenomenon from anomic aphasia?

Outside the Human Mind

There are other types of cognition than human. Animals exhibit behaviour we can call intelligent; just because they cannot express their thoughts in ways we understand does not mean they are not thinking. We will examine the ways in which we can study animal and what we have learnt from that. If we can learn enough about our own cognition, can we make something that thinks? The last few chapters in this book will look at the field of machine cognition, and what we can and cannot do with our knowledge of ourselves.

CHAPTER 15

Animal Cognition

Key terms

anthropomorphism the tendency to ascribe human characteristics to non-human entities, either animal or mechanical

ethology the study of behaviour, particularly animal behaviour, in the natural environment

evolutionary psychology an approach which attempts to show how psychological processes evolved by natural selection

insight learning the perception of relationships leading to solutions which can be applied in other settings, and which is unobservable

Key names

Darwin • Köhler • Miller • Mistlin and Perret • Mowrer and Mowrer • Premack and Premack

Why Study Animals?

Throughout the history of biological and psychological sciences we have learnt much from the study of animals. Some studies prevent the use of human participants because of moral and ethical considerations. This does not mean that it is always right to use animals, of course. The use of animals in research is an emotive area, and one which is quite rightly controlled. The British Psychological Society, which guides and monitors research in psychology, has set out guidelines which constrain the use of animals in experimentation and other types of research.[1] What we will consider in this chapter is the knowledge we have gained from the history of animal research.

The emergence of evolutionary theory in the 19th century led to the belief that the nature of human beings could be understood by studying animals. Darwin's view (1872) was that all species are biologically related, and the

[1]The guidelines and other details of the BPS can be requested by writing to The British Psychological Society, St Andrews House, 48 Princess Road East, Leicester LE1 7DR.

extension of that is that behaviour patterns must be related also. Humans differ from other animals only in complexity, so comparison is justified. Other justifications are based on convenience, as most species reproduce and mature more rapidly than humans, facilitating the study of the effects of early experience and selective breeding.

According to Miller (1985) there are many other benefits to both humans and animals that come from such research. Using classical conditioning techniques, Mowrer and Mowrer (1938) developed effective treatments for nocturnal enuresis. This gave benefits beyond the bladder control produced, in that children with behavioural and personality problems improved considerably once bed wetting had stopped.

Using operant conditioning techniques, pigeons have been trained in life saving. They were trained to detect life rafts, and were taken out by search and rescue helicopter crews to assist in searches (Simmons, 1981).

Other studies on classical and operant conditioning, which were carried out on animals, have been used to assist with the diagnosis and treatment of various mental disorders. Without such research, several modern theories and applications would not have been developed.

The major contribution that animal studies make is in the biological approach to psychology. If animals are biologically similar, then biological responses should be similar. Cognitive Psychology finds it more difficult to make this argument, but as there are biological, developmental and neurological models of cognition, then the comparative approach can be valuable.

There are of course difficulties in this work. Many argue that humans are not just quantitatively different from animals, but also qualitatively. There is also the problem of objectivity, as many researchers may fall into the trap of *anthropomorphism* and imbue their animal subjects with human properties. Many animal studies are laboratory based, and may lack ecological validity. Rossi (1992) also points out that not all species may be suitable for studying human behaviour, particularly cognitive processes. It should be stressed that there are alternatives to animal studies, such as *in vitro* techniques (for medical research), computer simulation, and, if animals must be studied, the use of an *ethological* approach – studying them in their natural habitat with the minimum of intrusion.

So, given that there are arguments about the practicalities and benefits of animal research, what have we learnt about animal cognition? There are limitations to what we can study with animals in Cognitive Psychology. The next few sections describe a few of the areas in which animals have been used.

Information Processing

The evolutionary approach to psychology suggests that organisms are sensitised to certain kinds of information and its processing because of innate factors. In other words, the capacity to process information was evolved through natural selection. Those of our ancestors who were more able to make sense of their environment were more likely to survive and pass on their genes to the next generation. Studying the way in which primates deal with the environment allows us, according to this evolutionary approach, to extrapolate to our own condition and develop sociobiological hypotheses to examine.

Perception

The neurological basis for perception is well established. Hubel and Wiesel's (1962) work on single neurone firing in the visual cortex was carried out using cats. There are many similarities between human and feline functions, particularly in vision (White, 1992), and this work is seen as seminal research in the area of perception. Knowledge of perceptual interruption was also enhanced by studying the cortical responses of monkeys (Mistlin and Perret, 1990). Neurones react differently to stimuli that were expected and unexpected in both visual and tactile areas of the cortex. Such findings have added much to our understanding of the perceptual process.

Communication

There has been much argument about whether exchanges between animals are simply mechanical. Empirical studies suggest that signals are contextualised, and that monkeys use quite distinct and specific calls to warn of the presence of different types of predators (Owings and Hennessy, 1984). The repertoire of communication is also larger than at first thought, and much more varied (Beletsky et al., 1986).

Evolutionary approaches account for this richness by suggesting that individuals will seek to control the behaviour of others (warning signals, for example, will produce particular responses).

Given that animals do communicate, some studies have sought to enhance our understanding of language acquisition and development in humans by studying it in primates. Chimpanzees can be taught an impressive array of non-verbal signals such as lexigrams (geometric symbols representing concepts and relationships) or sign language. Premack and Premack (1972) taught a chimp to use 130 symbols with about 80% accuracy and Savage-Rumbaugh (1990) showed that chimps can communicate with each other, not just their trainers, using sign language. Some researchers have concluded that chimps have similar linguistic abilities to bound children (the one-word and two-word utterance stages). However, it does appear that the use of language is different in that chimps signal for things they want and children will use language to explore, or to announce intentions (Seidenberg and Petitto, 1987).

Chimps do not appear to be capable of the full use of human language (but humans are unlikely to fully understand the language of other species, either).

Learning and Problem Solving

Much of the early work in learning was carried out using animals. Pavlov used dogs, and Skinner used rats and pigeons (see Chapter 12). Such studies have translated, at least partially, to theories of human learning. Complex learning, however, is more difficult to study. In Chapter 12 we discovered how rats can be shown to develop cognitive maps via latent learning, and again extrapolate to human cognition. One area where animal studies have been useful is in insight learning. In the 1920s Köhler set chimps problems in which the solution was readily available, but had to be sought. Previously animal studies had involved situations where the workings of the problem were invisible to the animal. Skinner's pigeons, for example, were never shown how to work the mechanism which gave them grain. Köhler's chimps were able to obtain bananas, which were placed out of reach, by using objects in the room as tools. This sometimes involved quite complex manipulations of the environment, such as building towers from boxes, and using multiple sets of sticks. We see something similar in several game shows on TV, but the contestants are not chimpanzees, and the prizes perhaps not as desirable as the banana to the ape.

The performance of the chimps in these situations is demonstrating complexity completely unlike the situation we see with accidental learning in Skinner boxes. In the latter, the solution was found by trial and error, or accident as with Thorndike's cats. With Köhler's chimps the solution was found suddenly, almost with an 'Aha!'. Once the chimp had found the solution, it would always repeat the actions without redundancy in movement, and it would transfer this learning to new problems. This indicates a mental operation, which leads to manipulation of the representation. The 'suddenness' of the solution is due to the internal action of the chimp's operation, which is not observable. The outcome of this was the theory that complex learning is a two-phase process: problem solving derives a solution, which is then stored in memory. Thus Köhler's work with chimps has led to a great deal of hypothesising and speculation about the nature and development of human learning. Not only that, but the two-phase theory has been used in Artificial Intelligence programs (Rosenbloom et al., 1991).

Summary

What is clear is that there is an unfinished debate about animal cognition, with a possibly erroneous emphasis on verbal ability. As Pinker (1994) puts it, humans may not be the only intelligent entities in the Universe. Simply because we cannot communicate with other creatures, and they do not appear to be self-aware and to think in the same way as we do, does not mean we should dismiss their experience. How often have we made this chauvinistic mistake when considering fellow human beings? There is also an argument to extend such broad-mindedness to non-organic creatures. We shall explore this idea further in the next two chapters on machine cognition.

Self-test Questions

1 Can animal research aid and benefit research in human psychology?
2 What aspects of animal behaviour have given us meaning for our own?

Machine Cognition

Key terms

computer simulation attempts to mimic human behaviour and environments using computers

metatheory an overarching theoretical approach to research questions, such as information processing

physical symbol system a system capable of storing and interpreting symbols

strong AI the view that computers may have mental states and hence be intelligent

Turing Machine an abstract machine which can read and write symbols, and change its internal state as a result

Turing test a competitive method devised for identifying true AI

Universal Turing Machine a Turing Machine which can carry out the processes of any other, given the same instructions

weak AI the view that computers are only symbol manipulators, and whilst a useful tool for studying the mind, cannot be intelligent

Key names

Newell and Simon • Norman • Searle • Turing • Weizenbaum

We can define Cognitive Psychology as the scientific study of mental processes and behaviour. One way of studying this is to reproduce it in a controlled environment, either with human participants in the laboratory, or by using simulated environments. An obvious evolution of this is to develop those environments in their own right. The study of animal cognition can tell us much about how humans developed; the study of machine cognition can tell us about how we function now, and in the future. Machine cognition, or Artificial Intelligence (AI), can be defined in one way as an approach to understanding cognition by reproducing it, so in this way it is closely linked to psychology. The means of reproducing it is via machines, and the best machines for this are computers. So AI is a joint effort between psychologists and computer scientists. The best people suited to this venture are those with a depth of understanding in one field, and knowledge of the other.

The history of AI shows some antagonism between the two approaches until the 1970s when a new hybrid discipline called Cognitive Science was developed. There has been such a growth in this area that if you wish to study psychology and understand the latest work in perception and cognition, then you must understand at least the basis of AI.

There are some difficulties in defining AI, not least because, as we know, there are problems defining intelligence. The term AI suggests that researchers continue to study certain kinds of behaviour like game-playing and solving puzzles. This was true of 'old' AI, but whilst working on these, techniques were developed allowing the study of other areas. These are the ones we will concentrate on, together with an examination of the arguments surrounding AI.

History of AI and Relationship to Cognitive Psychology

The goal of AI is to understand intelligence and hence to build machines that appear to be intelligent. So it is both a theoretical science and an applied one. The theoretical approach is akin to the philosophical approach to psychology, and they both share the same wishes. AI is strongly influenced by the information processing approach and in turn influences it. Much of AI looks at problem solving. In 1963 Newell and Simon developed a program called the General Problem Solver (GPS) that they said could solve mathematical theorems. This was use of computer simulation, copying human behaviour. It was a good attempt to produce computer behaviour that looked intelligent, but was simply a reproduction. However, certain methodologies were developed during this period that are still used in AI and psychology. Research is often intuitive in nature – we have an idea and construct studies to examine it. However, the more usual way is to start with a theoretical approach that suggests findings should be examined under controlled conditions. The third way of carrying out research is probably the most common in AI, and is known as *metatheory*. This is a schema for theory building, and an example is the information processing approach. Metatheory guides researchers in constructing theory. It is obviously an important element in Cognitive Psychology, but also for AI. Newell and Simon (1976) proposed the idea of a physical symbol system. These are systems that have the capacity for storing and interpreting symbols, such as humans, and computers. AI researchers believe that physical symbol systems have common elements, which means that we can examine all forms of intelligence in terms of these common characteristics.

Norman (1980) stated that there are several unifying problems with which science is concerned, and that we should make use of evidence from many branches of science to guide the development of another. If this is the case, then we can study cognition by constructing our theories without being limited by the imaginary boundaries between science.

The next stage of research is empirical investigation. Again AI is guided by Cognitive Psychology, but differs in that it is not limited by the characteristics of the human system. AI will mimic the process of cognition. In both areas the outcome of research is to build models; in psychology the models are the verbal descriptions we have been examining, in AI this is often a computer program. Accounts of what computations are possible by physical symbol systems is the mathematical theory of computability. There are two approaches to this. One is that computers will never actually think, but simply imitate. The other is that if computers interact with the world in the way people do, then this is, to all intents and purposes, thinking. Searle (1980) called this latter idea 'strong AI' and says we simply do not ascribe intelligence to the overt behaviour of entities, but also because of their biology, a view some term 'protoplasmic chauvinism'. Intelligent computers, it is thought by those who agree with Searle, pose danger to society in that (a) the mechanistic view of people is dehumanising, and (b) intelligent computers are a threat.

Let's look at the background to this. Mathematical computability theories have been around since the 1930s. They specify what computers do, and how much time and memory is needed for the tasks. One such theory was developed by Turing (1936). An abstract computing device was postulated called the Turing Machine. This performs calculations via tape holding symbols. The machine performs primitive operations by reading and writing symbols on the tape. The vocabulary of symbols is finite, but the tape is infinite. Reading a symbol may change the internal state of the machine, so affecting the nature of how to deal with subsequent symbols. The structure of the machine is simple, as are its operations. It is possible then to describe a Universal Turing Machine, which can mimic the operational behaviour of any other Turing Machine by being given a description of the machine in standard Turing format. This is arguably like any general purpose digital computer. The computer, running a program, behaves as if it were a machine for performing just that one task. In other words, it is an attempt to capture the notion of *effective procedure*.

> primitives or primitive operation basic units or actions that cannot be broken down into smaller units

> effective procedure one which can be carried out by a system without human intervention, and the outcome of which does not depend on intuition

Turing conjectured that any effective procedures could be carried out by his abstract machine. This is known as Turing's thesis, and has far-reaching implications for psychology. If Turing is correct, and psychological processes are not mysterious and are the subject of legitimate study, then we can describe those processes computationally. The other point is, if we can describe our processes computationally, we can describe computer processes psychologically, and the difference between us is simply one of biology. Turing considered the last point in detail. His original papers were published in the late 1930s. The following few years he was occupied with something else (the Second World War, and his code breaking work in the War Office).

However, in 1950 he finally got round to considering the question 'can machines think?'. He devised a test which he said could establish the answer when we were ready.

Turing's Test

Turing's test for establishing whether or not we have built true AI is based on an older game. Three people play the game: X and Y (one of whom is a man, the other a woman) are asked questions by a third (Z). X and Y are hidden from Z, and only communicate by some means which does not disclose their personal characteristics. Z must find which is which, but can use no other means than questioning these hidden people to disclose their identities. One of X or Y can give helpful answers, the other attempts to fool the interrogator, who does not know who is helpful and who is attempting deception. In this situation it is very easy to fool Z. Turing asked what would happen if a machine took the place of the person who is attempting to deceive. If it then fools the interrogator as often as a person can, the suggestion is that we should admit the machine is intelligent.

This test has never actually been set up, but there are claims that it has been passed by computers, 'accidentally'.

In 1966 Weizenbaum produced a program called ELIZA which plays the part of a psychotherapist. ELIZA works by picking out particular elements from sentences typed in by a person in the 'client' role, and using the elements in replies under specific rules. 'She' was well established when the following incident described by Bobrow (1968) took place.

ELIZA was running on a computer in a building where people habitually contacted each other via links on their computer terminals. A business manager tried to contact the programmers – and somehow got ELIZA. This exchange took place:

Manager: Do you think I can use the computer this morning?
ELIZA: Why do you ask?
I might be able to make some additional sales.
Why aren't you sure?
My prospective customers have never seen a demonstration of the system.
Does this mean very much to you?
Of course it does.
You seem very positive about that.
This is ridiculous.
What do you mean this is ridiculous?
Is there any reason why I can't use the computer now?
Tell me more about your prospective customers.

At which point the irate manager telephoned the programming office, and, on reaching an innocent and bewildered programmer, had this exchange:

Why the **** are you being so ***** with me?
What do you mean, why am I being so ***** with you?

It was subsequently claimed that ELIZA passed the Turing test. But the specifications were not met – it is intended to be a competitive situation, and the manager wasn't exactly attempting to distinguish between machine and person. The test is harder when the specifications are met, because, in a non-competitive set-up, certain things might be overlooked. In fact, no machine has been examined under the strict specifications.

The Turing test has been accepted as the most valid way of assessing AI. However, there are a few objections to this idea:

1 There is little doubt that several species besides adult humans can think. The few that spring to mind are chimps, dolphins and pre-linguistic babies. But these would all fail the Turing test, suggesting it is too conservative. If such 'intelligent relatives' fail the test, then a computer might too – even a truly intelligent one – simply because its responses are distinctively non-human. So a negative result in the test demonstrates no proof.

2 The test only concentrates on verbal responses, which means that the words are not examined with respect to their meaning. So the test could be passed without true understanding, and it is too liberal. Perhaps equipping the computer with artificial sense organs would remedy this? This would only test the understanding of concrete objects – wave a bouquet in front of artificial eyes and the computer might respond 'flowers – how sweet!'. But abstract concepts cannot readily be tested. So the computer would still fail. Adding such a specification would make it too conservative again.

3 Many would say simulation is still fake. Does it mean a computer thinks, if it can pass the test? All we know is that it looks like it is thinking. Go back to the original form of the game. Suppose that over a sufficient number of trials the man forces the wrong identification, and the interrogator thinks the man is a woman. This doesn't mean he *is* a woman, but can give a good simulation during conversations (so New Man does exist!). This argument would suggest that a computer might pass the test, but only as a fake human. This is spurious. Equip a machine with a simulated voice: it is artificial, but it is a voice. Simulation here is used with a different meaning to when we say simulated leather. Simulated leather replaces real leather, but is composed of different molecules. A simulated voice is just artificial, not produced by the same means, but it is not a fake.

4 A final objection concerns the 'black box' idea (from behaviourism, not the aircraft industry). A black box is judged entirely on its observable

behaviour, and no consideration is taken of internal workings or state. Behaviourists would say that this is entirely justifiable. However, when we judge another person's behaviour we do so on the basis that we are biologically similar, and we cannot do this with a computer. Once we know that the entity with which we are conversing is a machine, we revise our conclusions. This means it is still possible for a machine that does not think, and is merely a result of clever programming, to pass the test.

Is the test valid? Probably not. Things that do think might fail, things that do not understand the symbols might pass, the concept of simulation is erroneous, and again, things that don't think might pass. Perhaps we should not be trying to make machines that can pass such a test, but concentrating on what we *can* get machines to do. In the following chapter we will examine the psychological theories that have been put to work on developing machinery that can perform to its best abilities. Rather than ask 'can machines be intelligent?', we should be asking 'can they perform any or all of the functions that humans do, which we identify as intelligent behaviour?'

As in psychology we can list the areas of research in terms of information entering and leaving a system:

▶ Vision
▶ Memory and knowledge representation
▶ Problem solving
▶ Language

The next chapter will deal with each of these areas briefly.

Self-test Questions

1 What are the major difficulties in carrying out research in AI?
2 What is the Turing test, and why is it problematic for AI?
3 What value does the information processing approach have for work in AI?

CHAPTER 17

Machines and Cognitive Functioning – Can Computers See, Talk or Think?

Key terms

2½-D sketch the representation derived from the primal sketch, showing all the three-dimensional information that is available in the image

BLOCKSWORLD a miniature world of prismatic solids used to test the efficacy of vision processing programs

computational theory of vision a theory of vision derived from the information processing approach

grey-level description a computer held description of image boundaries

machine learning the acquisition of new knowledge in order to improve performance

monotonic reasoning reasoning based on the assumption that once a fact is verified it cannot be altered during the reasoning process

non-monotonic reasoning reasoning using multiple lines of thought allowing new facts or changed facts to be incorporated on the basis of new information

parsing syntactic analysis of sentences

phone spoken phoneme

predicate calculus a formalised logical language

primal sketch a cartoon-like description derived from the grey-level description

shape from shading apparent structure derived from drawn shading

stereopsis visual images from two eyes

structure from motion images are easier to see in motion

Key names

Evans • Fodor and Pylyshyn • Hillis • Marr • McClelland and Rumelhart • Mitchell • Schank and Abelson • Ullman

If we are to have truly intelligent machines, however we attempt to recognise this, then there are certain basic cognitive functions they must perform. This chapter looks at the possibility of just three: seeing, talking and thinking.

Can Computers See? The Work of David Marr

The area of artificial vision has been difficult to research and has minor successes in comparison to other fields. This in turn has led us to suppose that human vision is not the simple matter we have thought. Using the information processing approach, vision can be viewed as a series of steps. This is the computational model produced by, among others, Marr in 1982. These steps are processes that abstract information from the world and add it to the pattern created by previous steps. They are illustrated in Figure 17.1. This is a relatively simple model, but each stage involves a huge amount of computational minutiae. It has been quite successful, and there are robotic systems that appear able to incorporate them. There appears to be little relation to the research on human visual processing. This is one of the major differences in research: the psychological research has influenced the AI, but the latter then goes on to implement it in a way that works.

Vision is a high-level process; recognition of objects is necessary for the access and use of knowledge. The visually impaired use appropriate alternative techniques for perception, but still gain input from the visual world. Research in machine vision has two possible outcomes: programs with the

Figure 17.1 *Marr's computational model*

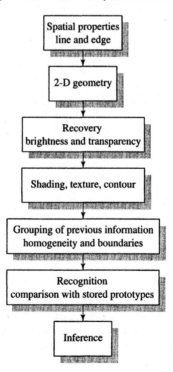

ability to process visual information, and aiding the repair and/or replacement of damaged human vision. Marr's work has concentrated on how the visual system builds descriptions of shapes and locations from images. Images are information entering the visual system when light is reflected from objects. The light is absorbed by the retinal receptor cells. There are three main types of visual processing of interest to AI.

Visual Processing Stages

Grey-level Description

This is a representation of the image in terms of edges. For each point in the visual field the intensity of light from the corresponding direction in space is encoded. This discovers boundaries, which occur where there is a sharp transition from light to dark. The problem in computer terms is in determining what is sharp. Marr assumed that these transitions are identified by local computations.

Primal Sketch

This is the representation derived from the grey-level description. It is a cartoon-like description, a line drawing, a collection of edges detected.

$2\frac{1}{2}$ -D Sketch

There is next a representation derived from the primal sketch. It shows all the three-dimensional information that is available in the image, i.e. the back of the image would not be available, neither would absolute distance.

The $2\frac{1}{2}$ -D sketch is very important. It includes various elements of vision which are significant if computer vision is to be successful.

Stereopsis is the component of vision derived from having two eyes with slightly different views. Stereoscopic images give depth information to the visual system without being three-dimensional in nature. For example, looking through '3-D spectacles' fools the eyes into viewing 2-D images as solid, likewise those random dot stereograms that are claimed to have hidden pictures in them. The apparent success of these means that stereoscopic identification of surface depth can be made before recognition of images has happened, allowing derivation from the primal sketch, and allowing computer vision to be built.

Moving objects are easier to see. Ullman (1979) showed how the visual system can work out *structure from motion*. For example, consider an object covered in spots, which is then filmed so that only the spots are visible. It is impossible to see it until it moves.

The other aspect that the sketch contains is *shape from shading*. Pen and ink drawings, for example, use shading to give the impression of depth, and depend on how the light is hidden or reflected. Shading is used before recognition.

So sophisticated elements of the image can be identified before it is recognised, therefore the process is data-driven. Computation of a 3-D image must contain information about the object's identity, implying the use of stored knowledge. Marr argued that humans can recognise things from stick figure representations, or even better, generalised cylinders. The 2½-D sketch can compute the necessary information from a stored catalogue of generalised constructions. This was studied in a series of miniature worlds, the best known of which was BLOCKSWORLD, built at MIT. BLOCKSWORLD showed how successful programs could be at identifying objects.

Discussion

Does this all mean that computers can see? If we are to create a completely intelligent machine, the ability to process information from the visual world is essential. Marr's work has allowed us to identify low-level and higher-level processing that can be broken down to primitive enough sub-processes to program. The computational theory describes vision with enough mathematical precision to allow computers to process visual information. But is it seeing? The argument of strong versus weak AI again crops up here. Just because computers can deal with visual information, it does not mean they are understanding it and processing it in the same way humans do. The links to all other aspects of storage and function in humans are much more complex than the computer models suggest, and there is some debate about vision versus seeing.

The next stage we will look at is communication with machines. If machines can perceive, then they and we must be able to communicate this fact.

Machine Communication – Can Computers Talk?

A major goal in AI is to have machines that can hold conversations, that is understand spoken language and speak in response to it. The problems here are large, and research progresses quite slowly. The areas examined are firstly speech (automatic speech recognition and speech synthesis), parsing (methods and types) and comprehension. In Chapter 14 we looked at several of these elements from the human point of view; now let's examine them from a machine perspective.

Speech

Speech-processing research concentrates on speech waves and phonemes, and there are two aspects, speech recognition and speech synthesis.

▶ Speech recognition – identifying words from properties of a speech wave.
▶ Speech synthesis – production of words from specifications of words and phonemes together with information about syntax and intonation.

These areas can be very technical, and the following is only an overview.

Speech research in AI was influenced by signal processing engineering work and we find programs written in the languages suitable for physical science and engineering. The programs are concerned with the methods of storing and using a continuous signal, like a speech wave. This involves making a digital copy of an analogue signal, without losing information. In a computer, the digitisation of speech is equivalent to a good telephone line with respect to maintaining information. It is, however, unlikely to be the way in which speech processing happens in humans, as signal storage takes a huge amount of memory and would only be acoustic in nature, not linguistic. Later systems go beyond this signal processing concept.

Automatic speech recognition attempts to provide labels for speech input, the label being a transcription of input as words or phonemes. The intended goal is to provide *real-time* (as it happens) transcription of natural speech. Programs identify a relatively small amount of words, though, and they must be spoken clearly and by a limited number of speakers. Human speech varies in many ways: think of accents, different genders, even how illness can affect your voice. Computers use template matching to recognise words, but it is unlikely that we do this since we have too large a vocabulary. Words have the smallest components that could be used to build a more efficient library anyway. The number of words or sentences in a language is limited only by imagination and ingenuity in using that language. The number of phonemes, however, is limited. In the same way as a very basic and small set of musical notes has led to the huge variety of music in the world, putting together speech sounds leads to potentially infinite variety of linguistic output.

In the USA a great deal of work was done on a project in ARPA (Advanced Research Projects Agency – part of the Department of Defense). They concentrated on speech *understanding*, and instead of attempting to write programs that could correctly identify masses of words, they concentrated on programs that understood a limited vocabulary. The computers, to be successful, responded correctly to input rather than transcribing – a pretty radical change in thinking about articulate speech. Several programs met the criteria of the ARPA project, but of course this is very limited. The other aspect of speech processing is speech synthesis. True synthesis is not simply reproduction of something stored as a digital signal, but is the production of words from true linguistically coded information. There are two basic techniques:

1 Described by Holmes *et al.* (1964), the first method is a technique of defining a spoken phoneme (called a phone) by a pattern of sound characteristics, and making a word from strings of phones. There are two problems with this: firstly, how to select patterns for every instance of a phone in any context, and secondly, how to decide to string phones together. This can be minimised by the second technique.

2 Diphone analysis (Isard and Miller, 1986) uses the links between phones as the point of reference, rather than the phones themselves. This forms a library of sounds which is easier to create from natural speech.

However, synthesised speech still sounds unnatural. It lacks the natural timing and intonation of human speech. In English, for example, although stresses on syllables are equally spaced, unlike many other languages, there is still variation and the length of spoken sound varies. Many other languages use intonation and stress to confer meaning and context. So we still have a long way to go in programming machine speech that sounds human. The question is: do we want it?

What we have discussed so far relates to the identification and reproduction of words, but not understanding. This would have to be based on groups of words, phrases, clauses and sentences. The way in which these are identified is a process called parsing, which we encountered in the chapters on language.

Parsing

Parsing identifies language in hierarchical groups of syntactic structures or *phrase markers*. In AI parsing has been quite important. Early programs attempting to understand languages used several different techniques.

Pattern matching was used by ELIZA and produced quite realistic conversations (see Chapter 16). But ELIZA did not understand what was being said.

General parsing methods usually use the left–right method used in Western reading, and also incorporate the type of decision tree seen in problem solving programs. It was later discovered that such generalised techniques could not guarantee to parse a sentence in a finite time, so heuristic techniques were also incorporated (see below). Such a program uses *augmented transient networks* (ATN) parsing developed by Thorne *et al.* (1968). The ATN is a network of nodes and links which represent common syntactical structures found in English, such as 'noun phrase followed by verb phrase'. As well as a realistic way of representing human parsing, ATN has been used successfully in computers, including a program that compiled information about lunar rocks and answered questions about them (Woods, 1977).

Other successful parsing techniques include chart parsing and Marcus parsing. Chart parsing stores sets of rules about grammar; charts hold possible syntactic analysis and agenda hold tasks to perform on them. Marcus parsing (Marcus, 1980) attempts to make parsing as efficient as human linguistic processing by limiting searches through possible analytical results.

Such techniques, however, still do not incorporate understanding. They are all based on syntax. Semantic parsers attempt to incorporate 'semantic grammars' as proposed by Schank and colleagues. These compare analysis to templates stored in the computer. However, errors in interpretation are still happening.

Comprehension of text and dialogue is still perplexing AI researchers. It requires, in human terms, a large amount of knowledge about the world, which we have not yet succeeded in getting computers to acquire in efficient forms. Realistically, artificial language will be achieved only when we have efficient linguistic analysis and can store a great deal of world knowledge in computers. Conversely, researchers in knowledge representation state that we cannot have human-like reasoning in computers until they can process language like humans. One way out of this circle might be supplied by connectionist approaches. Early work by McClelland and Rumelhart resulted in a model identifying letters and words (1981) and led to Seidenberg and McClelland producing a model which could read print and pronounce it (1989). This last model also exhibits the same pattern of reading difficulties, after connections are cut, as humans with surface dyslexia. Lei (1991) appears to have proposed a model of natural language comprehension combining a parallel comprehension of syntax and semantics, which has been simulated on computer. Cullinan *et al.* (1994) have also simulated the way in which children's language undergoes transition from two-word to three-word utterances. However, Fodor and Pylyshyn (1988), in a major criticism of connectionism, suggest that meaning will still be impossible with connectionism.

A final thought about artificial language: whilst we can appreciate AI's attempt to produce natural language processing and production in computers, and the values such machines would have in use (particularly by non-experts) when it has been achieved, what would those machines say to *us*?

Logic and Thought – Can Machines Think?

The final point about machine cognition is the most difficult. We find it hard to access our own thought processes, and simulating them and measuring them in an 'alien' environment is even harder.

Moving through our imaginary chain of information again, once information is in, it must somehow be stored and represented. Here we find a lot more collaboration between the disciplines concerned. A major theoretical development has been the representation of information in generalised but structured forms. In 1977 Schank and Abelson formulated the *script* as a plausible model for organisation and retrieval of information. This can be represented in computer terms via the Conceptual Dependency theory (Schank, 1975). This proposes a series of primitives, which are assembled into longer/larger units via predetermined principles. This might sound simple, but there are a large number of primitives and their connections are subsequently myriad. Scripts are not the only way of modelling memory, but computerising them has been quite successful.

In order to use stored information effectively, a system must be able to solve problems. Humans encounter many sorts of problems every day. The processes by which we attempt solutions are not observable to us, and in AI the way to start is to formulate a problem as explicitly as possible. Psychology can identify those problems on which it is feasible to do this, and then attempt to apply the method of deconstruction. Focus, therefore, has been on problems that follow rules, such as mathematics and game-playing. Conceptualising solutions then becomes a construction of a search through possibilities. Effective search strategies, and finding them, is an important area in AI. Cognitive Psychology describes two strategies for helping with this – algorithms and heuristics.

> algorithm description of task
> heuristic a 'rule of thumb' developed from experience

Algorithms describe tasks or problems that are well defined. They are not always efficient. For example, an anagram can be solved by following an algorithm of arranging the letters in all possible combinations until a meaningful word is seen. This is obviously *not* what contestants on '*Countdown*' do! Heuristics, on the other hand, are more efficient, but do not guarantee a solution.

Studying the ways in which humans use logic means we can apply them to computers. In Chapter 10 we looked at formal logic and natural reasoning. How might these be represented in the computer?

In theory, any programming language can be used to write a program to carry out any function, but the structure of some makes certain functions easier to implement. Languages such as FORTRAN are very suitable for programming typical numerical computations, but most models of intelligent behaviour are abstract or non-numerical. They require the manipulation of symbols standing for words, events, objects, etc., and list-processing languages have been developed such as LISP. This is actually a very simple

> predicate calculus a logic system first devised by Frege (1879) to formulate arguments in more depth than propositional logic. Consisting of predicates, constant terms, variables, logical connections and quantifiers

language, but its simplicity is also its strength, as there are features built in to allow a clear programming environment. Perhaps the most commonly used language in AI, however, is PROLOG. This is based on predicate calculus, and as such is very useful.

Predicate calculus is a powerful way of expressing real-world concepts in a formalised language.

Predicate Calculus

Predicates are statements about items in relation to themselves or others, and which have value of either TRUE or FALSE when applied to specific arguments, for example *is_white* can have an argument *(lecture room wall)* which will have the value TRUE, but *is_white (lecture room chair)* is FALSE.

The arguments of the predicates here are constants, but arguments can be variables:

left_of (x, table) means something is to the left of the table

or functions:

meets (martin, sister(helen)) means that Martin meets the sister of Helen

Here sister(helen) is a function which can be substituted with the name of my sister.

Predicate statements can be expanded with connectives. ¬ corresponds to 'not', and when placed in front of a statement will negate it:

¬ *asleep(students)* means the students are not asleep

¬ is a one-place connective, and cannot join statements. However, these do:

∀ or ∪ means 'universal' (for all)

∃ or ∈ means 'existential' (for some)

⇒ means 'if – then', e.g. *made_of(moon,greencheese)* ⇒ *edible(moon)*

& means 'and'

V means 'or'

Try to translate this statement:

∀ *(x) (man(x))* ⇒ ∃ *(y)(woman(y))* & *loves (x,y))*

It means 'for all x, if x is a man, then there exists some woman (y) such that x loves y', or 'for every man there is a woman to love'.

So predicate calculus is a powerful way of expressing real-world concepts in a formalised language. The possibilities for programming those concepts into a computer are obvious. PROLOG allows us to program a machine to use stored knowledge under clear rules.

There some very simple rules in predicate calculus:

▶ Formation rules – specifying which strings of symbols are the basis of well-known formulae, and could be used to identify 'commonsense knowledge'.

▶ Inference rules – showing how formulae can be derived from others.

The rules are established at the outset of a project, and can be subsequently built upon, new inferences forming the basis of new rules. For example:

$$\forall \ x(is\_hot(x)) \Rightarrow burns\_skin \ (x) \ \& \ \exists \ x(fire(x))$$

translates as 'for all x, if x is hot, then x will burn the skin and some x are fire': a new inference can be produced that fire will burn. This could be useful if it is a mobile robot with artificial skin which could be damaged, that is being programmed.

Predicate calculus is consistent and complete, but represents monotonic reasoning.

mototonic reasoning if new facts are added to a knowledge system, the integrity of existing and following factors remains the same

non-mototonic reasoning new facts added to the knowledge system may contradict existing knowledge

Much of human reasoning appears to be non-monotonic in nature. If we have knowledge about typical dogs, then what happens when we meet Rover? Knowing Rover is a dog, we infer he has four legs, but Rover sadly got run over, and had a leg amputated. The new fact that this is a dog, but has three legs, contradicts the existing knowledge. AI gets round this by building in default values (dogs have four legs) and the use of qualifiers.

Without qualification the inference reverts to the default value, but we can then change the knowledge base to include normal state + probabilistic values (99% of dogs have four legs + Rover is not in the 99%).

The rules of logic mean nothing without a set of knowledge on which to apply them, though. We must be able to access the knowledge, and it must be acquired and stored in some way. Predicate calculus is a uniform representation, treating all facts in the same way, making general procedures the way to infer new information. Domain-specific knowledge that experts use is highly specific and non-uniform. Semantic networks and similar representations are more appropriate here. Collins and Quillian's Teachable Language Comprehender (TLC) can add new facts, and includes the ideas of the intersecting search and inheritance hierarchy. This means that a multiplicity of relations will be attached to any individual item presented to the network. Facts can be verified, but slowly, and this requires a huge amount of storage. The propositional model of representation is better, allowing the incorporation of procedural knowledge.

Such networks can be built from quite complex primitives, which are described epistemologically. *Epistemological primitives* (Brachman, 1979) describe the internal structures of concepts and their inheritance. In addition to this level of description, there are conceptual levels (where primitives become subsets of concepts and relations) and the linguistic level (the interface between conceptual primitive and natural language). Thus the network is more complex, but only because the minimum level of representation is allowed to be complex. Brachman incorporated this into a language called KL-ONE which was a knowledge representation language (not strictly a programming language) written in LISP. KL-ONE is a set of epistemological primitives describing relation between generic objects and/or individual concepts.

The inheritance of properties can be from distant nodes, making for extensive searches, and the network is probably tangled and multidimensional. Fahlman (1979) looked at how searches could be made more efficient. He came up with the virtual copy, i.e. that part of the network representing Rover should behave as if it contained a copy of the network part containing descriptions of dogs that are typical of his breed. Obviously, copies within copies is unmanageable, and Fahlman devised another language called NETL. This behaves as if it contains virtual copies, but is still unwieldy. Fahlman said it should be implemented on special parallel distributed processing (p.d.p.) hardware. This did not exist in 1979, and Fahlman was simulating the action of this parallel hardware on a serial computer. This gives us some idea of how researchers started to think about knowledge representation on computers. For a more detailed look at this subject, read Bench-Capon (1995).

The abstract network models of knowledge have therefore been very useful, but some knowledge is more easily represented as a set of production rules. In AI these are known as rule-based systems. A production states that given a set of conditions, then certain actions can be performed. New information can be added, but may form links, which cause conflicts. So these systems incorporate conflict resolution strategies. A separate procedure is not needed for each incident of using the knowledge, but generalised rules will take the place, with built-in 'safety mechanisms'. Using productions to make inferences can be by forward or backward chaining. Forward chaining starts from initial conditions and performs actions needed; this step creates a new set of conditions and so on, until the solution is reached. Backward chaining starts with the goal, matching it with actions to find the conditions that have to hold for the goal to be achieved. These ideas are reasonable representations, but cannot be readily implemented on serial machines. New developments in computer architecture, called Very Large Scale Integration (VLSI), involve putting more and more electronic components onto computer chips. The type of machine proposed by Fahlman would consist of millions of components. In 1985, Hillis proposed a prototype of such a machine called the *connection machine.*

Connectionism has been important in AI development. Connection machines store information as connections between simple elements. Some of these are localised representations of information with their own node. Other models employ distributed memories – a single item of information is presented as a pattern of associations and evoked rather than found. Hence information is retrieved in the form of relationships between units, rather than as the units themselves. This is known as content addressable memory, and can find information from partial descriptions, in the same way humans can. Connection machines are useful for formulating low-level processes.

Machine Learning

Real progress is unlikely in AI until machines learn. If the computers incorporated learning processes, much of the encoding and programming which is now necessary would not be needed, since the machines would do it themselves. The latest developments in this area are quite astounding, with the researchers themselves unsure of how the systems are learning.

There is a history of problems in this area of AI, with computer scientists questioning that the nature of intelligence depends on learning. Skills can be described without describing how they are learnt. Also, learning has been studied extensively under the behavioural paradigm, which cognitive scientists would find complete anathema! Modern thinking in AI, however, realises that we cannot get away with this rejection. Chapter 12 discussed the various types of complex learning, and these have been used to a certain degree in machines.

look ahead a game play technique where the current move is evaluated by looking ahead to possible subsequent moves; in practice this must be limited, or systems will spend too much time searching

static evaluation evaluation of board positions or card hands, etc., as to whether they are wins or losses, made on the basis of several factors

minimaxing a decision strategy in which the positions at the end of the look ahead are evaluated by static evaluation, and the consideration of the next move is then based on the assumption that the opponent will make the best for him or her

Learning by Being Told

We can not only learn facts from what we are told, and store them, but also gain advice, which turns into plans. A system designed by Mostow (1983) called First Operational Operationaliser (Foo) learns advice about card game playing and operationalises it into plans. Samuel's CHECKERS (draughts) program, written in 1963, also used standard game playing techniques such as look ahead, static evaluation and minimaxing. Samuel called the operation of CHECKERS either rote learning, in which board layouts are stored, or learning by generalisation, in which evaluation of layouts is used to improve chances of winning. Using both techniques the program was improved until it was at good competition standard.

Learning from Mistakes

HACKER (Sussman, 1975) was devised to solve planning problems in the BLOCKSWORLD. It learns by debugging plans that deviate from the expected solution. Initially HACKER knows the primitive for moving one block at a time, but learns to plan complex stacking, and plan modification. If plans fail, attempts are made to correct it, and subsequent failures add to the learning. It then adds these attempts to its answer library.

HACKER needs a teacher, who must set it problems carefully devised to become progressively more complex.

Learning by Example

Inductive learning works by generalising from facts and refining (specialising) these generalisations via further facts. Mitchell (1982) described learning by induction as a 'search problem' in which the 'search space' is the set of possible generalisations and the correct one must be found. This means that strategies for searching are needed. These include depth-first and breadth-first.

depth-first one hypothesis is used at a time to search through possibilities

breadth-first all possible hypotheses are tested against each instance

Breadth-first searching was extended by Mitchell (1982) into *version space* strategy – using the set of generalisations not already eliminated. An example of a system using this is LEX (Mitchell *et al.*, 1983). Such strategies are data-driven which means the set is only narrowed down as data become available.

Model-driven strategies use induction procedures – they select a hypothesis on the basis of what the world *should* be like, and test it. This is known as generate-and-test. Michalski's INDUCE 1.2 (1983) uses such a strategy.

Learning by Exploring

This means taking concepts already known to conjecture about new ideas. In the early 1980s, several programs by Lenat appeared to do this with mathematical concepts and allied domains. The major problem encountered with such concepts is that there is no clearly defined goal. However, some of the things that the programs have come up with are interesting and worthy of note in theoretical mathematics – Lenat (1983).

Connectionism

AI still leaves many questions about learning unanswered, particularly the fact that machines seem to need at least a basic set of concepts before they can learn new ones. Connection machines, though, do seem to learn without relying on in-built concepts. They learn to classify objects as belonging or not belonging to the category or class when presented with members or non-members and told which is which. The ability to classify is encoded into links between the processors, links being those that are excited or inhibited. The strength of the links changes in response to training. So a connection machine *builds* its concepts from very basic primitives.

The strength of the links is adjusted according to several in-built rules. These rules can lead to what Rumelhart and Zipser (1985) described as competitive learning – an exciting development as this would not require a teacher.

Connectionist models of learning are again seemingly acting very closely to how the brain works, even to the extent that if they are damaged they seem to mimic the consequences of brain damage (Hinton *et al.*, 1993) in much the same way that language models mimic dyslexia (see above).

Learning, then, can take many different forms, and AI has attempted to program them. What we need to examine now is the way in which AI has used the possibility of a learning machine to make a thinking machine.

Artificial Thinking

Thinking has been examined in several categories:

Problem solving   – competitive and non-competitive
                     – search for solutions
Theorem proving – resolution
                     – rules
                     – proofs
Planning   – systems

Problem Solving

Research on problem solving looks at how solutions are found, rather than creative thinking. For example, in many IQ tests we will find the following type of problem. There are three geometrical figures: **A, B** and **C**. **C** has several possible configurations. You have to decide which configuration of **C** is related to **B** in the way **B** is to **A**. In 1968, Evans described a program called ANALOGY (because it was using analogical reasoning) which succeeded in solving such puzzles. It does so by breaking down the figures into components and determining relationships like *Rotation, Reflection*, etc. This is a bit of a sledgehammer technique, but successful, if limited.

> missionaries and cannibals a logic puzzle in which the task is to transport three missionaries and three cannibals across a river in a boat, which needs at least one person to propel it across the river, but holds only two people. If at any time the cannibals outnumber the missionaries on either bank, the missionaries will be eaten

AI also looks at the difference between competitive and non-competitive problems (games with two adversaries or one player). Adversarial games are those like chess, non-adversarial those maddening logical puzzles like missionaries and cannibals.

Finding solutions involves searching through possibilities. ANALOGY evaluates all possibilities, but there is only a small number in its domain, and this search strategy is rare.

Searches are directed by control strategies which aim to seek either *any* solution, or the *best* solution. Simple depth-first or breadth-first strategies are often impractical and time-consuming, and so heuristic methods are used to focus attention on the optimal parts of the pathways (or 'trees') down which the searches go. Depth-first strategies include variations such as 'hill-climbing'. The search follows a single path, but there is an evaluation function determining the choice of path by how close the searcher can get to the solution in one step. Breadth-first variations include 'best-first', which again is evaluative, but examines where it has been rather than where it is going. Several programs have been devised that use such strategies.

Game playing also follows such strategies, but must evaluate what the next best move is, and hence must also use decision strategies. Game players must limit their look ahead to use time optimally, and to get the best move in comparison to the opponent.

Theorem Proving

Theorem proving is very formalised use of knowledge, and usually involves deductive reasoning, which can be represented by predicate logic. However, human theorem provers also use inductive reasoning requiring specialised knowledge, rather than generalised techniques.

The best-known programs in this area are those devised by Newell and Simon, such as General Problem Solver (GPS), etc. The research in GPS was intended to devise machines that could solve problems that require intelligence, and to build models of human problem solving. GPS incorporates general solution techniques which are separate from any specific domain-based knowledge. Due to this, its designers were sure it could solve any problem, as it would reduce the problem to initial and goal states, and navigate them using means–end analysis. Unfortunately, it didn't work in quite this way, but is a valuable contribution to the area.

Planning

When faced with problems of any nature, humans often plan ways of reaching solutions. Computer planning systems are often robotically based, and perform distinct physical actions. What is often shown here is how things can go wrong in the search exercise, and single actions can have multiple effects. There is a need to specify what will change as the result of an action, and what remains the same – this is known as the *frame problem*.

frame problem the inability of mental representations to model the effects of real actions

A system must also break down its goal into several sub-goals in order to decide upon, and perform, actions.

Learning and thinking in AI is a complex business. Knowledge must be stored and represented, and programs must be able to navigate and use this knowledge. Learning is important as we have realised that if a machine can learn, then this will minimise programming effort. The connectionist paradigm seems the best possibility so far.

Summary

This has been a long chapter, but has still only looked at the surface of theories and progress in AI, and essentially from a historical perspective. If you are interested there are many very good books on the market which will go a little further than we can here.

Self-test Questions

1 What value is derived from models of vision such as that proposed by Marr?
2 What aspects of the $2\frac{1}{2}$-D sketch suggest that recognition is unnecessary for visual processing?
3 What are the major difficulties encountered in attempting to produce systems that use natural language?
4 Why has so much work been done on attempting to produce a machine that can learn?

CHAPTER 18

Concluding Thought

Cognitive Psychology is, by its very nature, a science of the unobservable. Mental representations and skills can only be studied by inferring from behaviour. However, those laboratory experiments and in-depth neurological studies of patients do have real applications:

1 In human factors, findings of psychology can assist with the design of devices, and the evaluation of their use, and the investigation of failures. The human element in the operation of machinery is an important one, and comfort, ease of use and efficiency can be optimised by taking into account psychological factors.

2 Eye-witness testimony is an important piece of evidence in any forensic investigation, or legal procedure. Improvements in accessing such testimony, and correct identification, can be assisted by cognitive techniques and principles.

3 The study of mental processes has real implications for education. Understanding of how knowledge is acquired, retained and used can affect teaching and assessment methods.

4 Artificial Intelligence is a relatively new endeavour, which has benefited from the application of Cognitive Psychology. Understanding of human intelligence and cognitive functioning will aid the construction of alternative forms. Psychology brings rigorous research techniques to many areas, but together with this is the consideration of ethical implications.

5 Finally, cognitive impairments are one of the most distressing outcomes of accident and disease. Cognitive neuropsychologists are involved in the diagnosis and treatment of patients with such problems, due to the knowledge of attention, problem solving and psycholinguistics.

We have travelled through the cognitive system, following information as it impinges on our sense organs, becomes transformed into other meaningful forms, is stored and used. The information processing approach, however, is not the only one to which Cognitive Psychology subscribes. It also can give a false impression of humans as little pieces of functioning linked only by information. What we must bear in mind is that cognition, human, machine or that of the animals with which we share this world, is fascinating and its study is essential in many areas. There are many issues confronting cognitive science, more than have been presented in this book. Study well, and perhaps you will not only understand those issues, but help to meet the challenge.

Answers to Self-test Questions

Chapter 2

1 What is the perceptual threshold?
The point at which stimuli can be detected, absolute or differential.

2 How are associations formed?
From experience, two or more items become linked together. This forms cognitive associations fortuitously, which are then stored and recalled later.

3 Why do spoonerisms fail to support the behaviourist tradition?
Spoonerisms are examples of anticipatory errors, and refute the idea of associative chains.

4 In what ways can the simplicity principle be applied?
The simplicity principle states that we perceive things in their simplest unified form. Thinking and problem solving, as areas of study in Cognitive Psychology, can apply the principle to phenomena such as insight.

5 How is decision time calculated?
Reaction time for choices between two items is made up of two processes, detection and decision, so decision time is reaction time minus detection time. Detection time is found by comparing the reaction for one stimulus and the choice between two.

6 Has psychology influenced the design and use of machinery, or have the machines influenced the study of human cognition?
Machinery was initially designed with just function in mind. As errors in machine use were seen, there was evident need for studying how we use them, and how we can use them effectively. Cognitive Psychology has therefore grown out of a need, but has subsequently influenced design.

7 What are the three major problems with a traditional information processing approach?

The need for experimentation which is seen as lacking ecological validity, the lack of integration and a unified framework, and the idea of a person as a machine, or a system.

Chapter 3

1 Write down the process from detection of stimuli by the sense organs to detection in the brain, in vision, hearing and taste.
Stimuli affect a receptor by changing energy, which transduces into neural impulses, transmitted to cortex.
Vision: light – retinal cells (rods and cones) – transduction – optic nerve – visual cortex (feature detector sensitive to particular aspects).
Hearing: sound waves – receptors in middle ear (bones) – receptors in inner ear (fluid) – transduction – auditory nerve – auditory cortex.
Taste: molecules soluble in saliva – taste buds receptors – transduction – cranial nerves – hind-brain – thalamus and gustatory cortex – limbic system.

2 How do direct theories of perception differ from constructivist theories?
Direct theories assume the process of perception is data-driven, and all that is needed is the sensory information, whereas constructivist theories suggest that perception is a process of data and memory integration and interaction.

3 What can babies see?
Little detail until 6 months old, some colour and they can detect movement.

4 What evidence is there to support the idea that perception is organised?
We discriminate between figure and background, we can make sense of binocular and kinaesthetic cues to perceive depth, and size, colour and shape remain constant. We can also recognise patterns.

Chapter 4

1 Why are bottleneck theories of attention so called?
Bottleneck theories of attention assume that all the sensory information received will pass into the cognitive system, but that we cannot process it all. Therefore the material passes through a filter, and hence there is a bottleneck at which some information is lost.

2 What would be the effect of attenuation?
Instead of filtering out information, it is tuned down, and some low-level processing is still taking place, even though conscious attention is not being given to it.

3 Why are late selection models simpler than other bottleneck theories?

They do not depend on filters, or tuning down information; the latter appears to mean that attention is being given to all information. Late selection suggests that information is held, but the selection of material for active attention is later in the system.

4 How does the resource allocation policy of capacity models work?
Capacity is limited and there is a policy for allocating resources dependent on cognitive control and arousal.

5 What does the Stroop effect demonstrate about automaticity?
That processes which are so familiar as to have become automatic will override other instructions.

Chapter 5

1 What are the different forms of consciousness and how are they related to memory and awareness?
Anoetic consciousness is related to procedural memory, as this is a type of memory which works without awareness or attention; noetic consciousness is related to semantic memory as this type of memory involves awareness of knowledge; and autonoetic consciousness is related episodic or autobiographical memory, as this involves personal experience.

2 Why does habituation happen?
The repetitive stimulus will cause changes in the RAF, which is involved in arousal.

3 What evidence is there to suggest localisation of brain function with respect to attention?
Brain scan techniques show separate areas of the brain being activated in response to different attentional stimuli.

Chapter 6

1 What are the major distinctions between sensory store, transient store, and permanent store?
Sensory store is very limited in duration, with limited organisation and with material being inaccessible. Transient store is of limited capacity and fragile, with some organisation and with information being retrievable. Permanent store is durable and highly organised but subject to retrieval failure. Distinctions are in duration, accessibility and organisation of information in each type of store.

2 How can we demonstrate the serial position effect?
By asking participants to recall a list of words; on average they will remember the first (primacy) and last (recency) parts of the list better than the middle. The first part is thought to be in long term store, and

the later part still in short term, as the recency effect can disappear after distraction.

3 How would the levels of processing theory explain the fact that material can fail to reach long term store?
Material might not be encoded deeply enough with sufficient salience to achieve permanent storage.

4 What different types of information are handled by the phonological loop and the visuo-spatial sketch pad?
Phonological loop deals with verbal information, and the sketch-pad with visual information, or spatial descriptions (e.g. directions).

5 In what ways can permanent memory be categorised?
Permanent memory can be classified by
a) the form in which information is encoded, forming episodic (persona) or semantic (meaningful) memories
b) the form in which it can be used, whether as facts (declarative) or action (procedural)
c) the form in which it is reproduced, being explicit (related to cues) or implicit (cues 'forcing' retrieval).

6 Summarise the evidence that memory might have physical structure.
Removal of brain tissue eventually damages memory, leading to the conclusion that they are linked; specific stimulation of brain tissue will activate specific memories; modern brain scanning techniques show activation of brain areas when participants are using memory.

Chapter 7

1 Why might transient store codes not be wholly auditory in nature?
Verbal decisions take longer than acoustic ones, suggesting two processes are happening. Also release from proactive inhibition shows semantic coding is taking place.

2 What is the Sternberg paradigm?
An experimental procedure in which a probe is compared to a memory set, demonstrating that the participants compare the probe to the items in the set sequentially.

3 What might limit the transfer of information from transient to permanent store?
Prevention of encoding, poor depth of encoding, inappropriate type of encoding.

4 What are the differences between the processes occurring in recognition and recall?
Recognition is the comparison of cues with stored information, whereas recall is the production of one's own cues.

5 What are the differences between clustering and semantic networks?
Clustering suggests that memory is composed of groups of items placed in similarly based categories, whereas semantic networks suggest a hierarchical structure within the categories based on level of generalisability.

Chapter 8

1 What are the two theories of everyday forgetting?
Decay (memory traces simply deteriorate) and interference (memories compete for space).

2 What is the difference between retroactive and proactive inhibition?
RI means new information interferes with old, and PI means old information interferes with new.

3 What are the traumas with which amnesia is associated?
Head injury, degenerative diseases of the brain, metabolic disorders, often associated with alcohol abuse leading to thiamine deficiency, and psychogenic states resulting from negative life events.

4 What is the difference between anterograde and retrograde amnesia?
Anterograde amnesia is the inability to remember information after the onset of the disorder, the inability to learn new information. Retrograde amnesia is characterised by inability to remember information from before the onset.

5 What are the differences in the ways in which forgetting and amnesia are studied?
Forgetting happens to us all, and is studied via controlled environment laboratory experiments investigating isolated pieces of behaviour. Amnesia is studied by case study, and often each case demonstrates a unique pattern of memory loss. Experiments in forgetting can be done using manipulation of situations; amnesia must be studied after it has happened.

6 Why do these differences occur?
Experiments in forgetting can be done using manipulation of situations; amnesia must be studied after it has happened. We cannot 'cause' amnesia as this would be unethical.

Chapter 9

1 How would semantic priming be explained by the three major types of knowledge representation models – semantic, propositional and connectionist?
Semantic networks would suggest that priming happens because the presentation of a word triggers the part of the hierarchy in which it

resides; propositional networks suggest that the activation of two pieces of declarative knowledge together is due to the productive link between them; and connectionist models would suggest that the link itself is evoked, bringing about both items together.

Chapter 10

1 How do prototype and exemplar theories of concept formation differ?
Prototype theories suggest that all experienced examples of a category will be 'averaged' in terms of features to build a typical category member, whereas an exemplar is the most salient example of a category. Each theory suggests that the concept is formed on the basis of either its prototypical member or its exemplar member.

2 How might you demonstrate how to overcome functional fixedness?
By prior experience. If people are given the opportunity to carry out problem solving with non-fixed solutions, the next time such a problem is encountered, the experience will allow them to perform without being set in particular forms of function.

3 What is the difference between problem solving and decision making?
Decision making is the choice between several alternatives; problem solving is the process of finding a solution when there is no obvious method available.

Chapter 11

1 Why does the psychometric approach cause difficulties for Cognitive Psychological examination of intelligence?
Psychometric tests do not necessarily measure intelligence, and do not access the internal cognitive processes. Cognitive Psychological studies of intelligence can combine psychometrics with performance on cognitive tasks.

2 What are the major differences between stage theories and the information processing approach to cognitive development?
Stage theories assume that there is a progression from one level of ability to the other with an underlying use of logical structures. The information processing approach supposes development is via growth in the knowledge base and increasing automatisation of cognitive processes.

3 Write down as many uses for a brick as you can.
Well, how many did you get? Are your suggestions creative or merely original?

Chapter 12

1 What are the differences and similarities between classical and operant conditioning?
Classical conditioning proposes that the response is linked to a hitherto unrelated stimulus by repeated and often intentional pairings with related stimuli, whereas operant conditioning shows that learning can be by accidental pairings of stimuli and response which are then refined. Both theories use limited paradigms and suggest that learning is a simple linkage between environment and outcome. Both were based on animal experiments, suggesting that animals are incapable of complex learning or insight.

2 Why does the behavioural approach to learning not offer a full explanation?
There is no explanation for the role of cognitive processes. Latent learning in particular cannot be explained by behaviourism as it suggests learning which is not directly influenced by environment.

3 What can the cognitive approach tell us about learning?
Learners are active information seekers, and internal as well as external influences mediate behaviour and learning.

4 How might skills be acquired?
By understanding of task and use of strategies to allow perception and retrieval of information. Use of feedback reduces errors, and finally performance becomes automatic.

5 What differentiates experts from novices?
Level of knowledge, and structure of knowledge. Knowledge is highly organised, the boundaries are less distinct, and the knowledge is embedded in procedural rather than declarative structures. Performance is automated, experts can change strategies when required, and they know the limitation of their knowledge.

Chapter 13

1 What evidence is there to suggest the existence of a language acquisition device?
There is cultural invariability in language development; all children learn to use their native language at about the same time, and in the same general order. There are a small number of phonemes, even though they are used with great variability around the world. This cross-cultural similarity leads to a proposal of innate structures for language, suggesting a biological basis for language acquisition, with development mediated by environment and culture.

2 At what point is a child explicitly trying to communicate?

Probably from birth when needs are clearly being demonstrated. However, it is likely that the use of words rather than sounds signals the child's need to communicate using language.

3 Why is crying said to be a reflexive response rather than true communication?
Crying appears to be a response to an internal state, rather than recognition of external environment.

Chapter 14

1 Why might sentences not be the natural unit of spoken language?
Spoken speech does not always consist of complete sentences, and natural pauses occur at clause endings. When fluency of speech is examined, people express ideas in units other than sentences.

2 What are the stages of language processing?
Perceptual, analytical and representational.

3 What differentiates the TOT phenomenon from anomic aphasia?
TOT is experienced occasionally, and words can still be recovered by various structural strategies. Anomia, after brain damage, often means the words are never recovered.

Chapter 15

1 Can animal research aid and benefit research in human psychology?
Yes, it can, by helping to develop therapies in areas where human participants cannot be used, and by demonstrating the possible evaluation of cognitive processes.

2 What aspects of animal behaviour have given us meaning for our own?
Studies of perception, learning, communication and problem solving in animals have all aided study in human cognition.

Chapter 16

1 What are the major difficulties in carrying out research in AI?
The lack of a clear definition of intelligence, the lack of coherence in approach, and the concerns about simulation rather than building true intelligence. There is also the difficulty of recognising intelligence which may be different from our own.

2 What is the Turing test, and why is it problematic for AI?
A way of identifying when true AI has been achieved. The problems lie in the fact that non-intelligent entities, i.e. those which do not truly understand the functions they are performing, could pass the test, and

also entities which we identify as intelligent would fail due to the reliance on the use of human language.

3 What value does the information processing approach have for work in AI?
It provides a meta-theoretical framework within which to approach the questions of AI. The experimental paradigm and the theoretical approach can guide research.

Chapter 17

1 What value is derived from models of vision such as that proposed by Marr?
They allow us to study human vision, and have led to the conclusion that it is a more complex process than at first thought. If artificial vision is achieved, it may provide alternative solutions for the visually impaired.

2 What aspects of the $2\frac{1}{2}$-D sketch suggest that recognition is unnecessary for visual processing?
A computer system which can process a $2\frac{1}{2}$-D sketch will do so without any recognition of objects.

3 What are the major difficulties encountered in attempting to produce systems that use natural language?
Flexibility and novelty of language mean that not all possible combinations of words can be stored. Ambiguous meaning is also a problem.

4 Why has so much work been done on attempting to produce a machine that can learn?
If machines can learn, then much of the routine programming and knowledge input would be removed. We are unlikely to achieve a fully thinking machine until one can learn.

Glossary

2½-D Sketch. Representation derived from the primal sketch, showing all the three-dimensional information that is available in the image.

Accommodation. Modifying existing mental structures to fit reality.

Adaptive Control of Thought. A model of knowledge representation.

Anoetic Consciousness. 'Non-knowing' awareness of the current situation.

Anterograde Amnesia. Inability to encode new information following onset of a memory disorder.

Anthropomorphism. Tendency to ascribe human characteristics to non-human entities, either animal or mechanical.

Aphasia. Difficulties with spoken language after brain damage.

Articulatory or Phonological Loop. A component of working memory concerned with holding verbal information, of limited capacity, determined by temporal duration.

Assimilation. Interpretation of events in terms of present mental structures.

Associationism. A theory of cognitive functioning in which learning and thinking consist of a sequence of experiences linked via various principles.

Attention. Focus of mental effort on information reaching the cognitive system.

Attenuation. Tuning down information rather than tuning or filtering it out.

Autobiographical Memory. Memory of individual's past events.

Automaticity. When a process becomes so familiar one no longer needs pay attention to it.

Automatisation. Execution of mental processes with increasing efficiency.

Autonoetic Consciousness. 'Self-knowing' awareness associated with personal experience.

Behaviourism. A theory of functioning in which learning, thought and behaviour are the result of stimulus–response relations.

BLOCKSWORLD A miniature world of prismatic solids used to test the efficacy of vision processing programs.

Bottleneck Theories. Models of selective attention in which information must pass through an area where there is insufficient space for everything.

Brain Asymmetry. The different functions and awareness of the left and right brain hemispheres.

Capacity Model. Model of attention in which selection is carried out on the basis of resources rather than filters.

Central Executive. A component of working memory which may identify processes that are needed, and are involved in planning.

Centration. Focusing on one striking feature of an object and ignoring others.

Chunking. Reorganisation of material in transient store so that related items are processed together, and can be encoded more effectively.

Classical Conditioning. Learning in which an environmental stimulus produces a response.

Clustering. A form of organisation in permanent store.

Clustering Model. A model of knowledge representation in which concepts are stored together.

Cocktail Party Phenomenon. A situation where filtering is seen quite clearly, but also demonstrates that salient information will be processed.

Cognitive Economy. A feature of models in which items are stored with lack of redundancy.

Cognitive Interview. Interview with eye-witnesses designed to raise the integrity and amount of information gained.

Cognitive Map. A mental representation of a situation.

Cognitive Science. A discipline combining computer science, neuroscience and Cognitive Psychology.

Cognitive System. The structure that deals with information.

Computational Theory. A theory suggesting that cognition is a series of computable steps.

Computational Theory of Vision. A theory of vision derived from the information.

Computer Simulation. Attempts to mimic human behaviour and environments using computers.

Concept. Representation of items based on grouping by common attributes.

Connectionism. A theory of cognition allied to associationism, but which emphasises the strength and type of connection between elements.

Connectionist Model. Knowledge representation model in which knowledge is stored in terms of strengths of connections between items, also known as parallel distributed processing (p.d.p.) models.

Conservation. Understanding of stability of properties of objects.

Constructivist Theory. A theory suggesting that perception is the matching of input and stored memories, resulting in an amalgam of both.

Convergent Thinking. Thinking that involves previously used strategies or knowledge.

Creativity. Ability to produce valued outcomes in a novel way.

Critical Period. Biologically determined stage of organic and cognitive development during which language must be acquired.

Cue-Dependent Forgetting. Loss of retrieval cues leads to loss of information.

Decay. A theory of forgetting in which memory traces decay.

Decision Making. Process of making a choice between several alternatives based on the attractiveness and utility of each alternative.

Declarative Knowledge. Factual knowledge.

Deductive Reasoning. Reasoning based on sets of rules and logical relations between items.

Deep Structure. The underlying meaning of sentences.

Dichotic Listening. A way of studying auditory stimuli processing.

Direct Perception. A theory which supposes that all that is required for accurate perception is the sensory input, a data-driven theory.

Dissociative Amnesia. A psychogenic form of amnesia associated with trauma.

Dissociative Fugue. A psychogenic state involving almost total memory loss, and hence identity loss; often temporary.

Dissociative Identity Disorder. Multiple personality disorders associated with high levels of repression due to sustained trauma or abuse. Or faking.

Divergent Thinking. Generation of multiple useful possibilities from a given situation.

Dyslexia. Difficulties with written language, either developmental or acquired.

Ecological Validity. Ability to generalise results from a study across a variety of settings.

Egocentrism. Embedded in one's own point of view.

Electroconvulsive Treatment. Application of electric current to the head, producing convulsions and possible unconsciousness, used in the treatment of some mental disorders.

Eliza A computer program which uses simulated conversation to act as a psychotherapist.

Empiricism. Acquisition of knowledge through experience.

Equilibration. Balancing assimilation and accommodation.

Ethology. Study of behaviour, particularly animal behaviour, in the natural environment.

Evolutionary Psychology. An approach which attempts to show how psychological processes evolved by natural selection.

Exemplar. An example of a member of the concept which is the most typical.

Experimentation. A research approach in which attempts are made to identify causal relationships among variables under controlled conditions.

Expertise. A high level of skill, probably involving different types of pattern storage.

Filter Model. Channel of limited capacity in bottleneck theories.

Functional Fixedness. Tendency to view and use items in terms of usual functions.

'g'. General intelligence.

Gestalt Theory and Principles. German 'configuration': a theory which states that experience is coherent and unified.

Grey-level Description. A computer-held description of image boundaries.

Habituation. Lack of response seen on repetitive presentation of a stimulus.

Human Performance/Human Factors. A research approach based on studying the factors which affect performance.

Inductive Reasoning. Reasoning based on prior experience and beliefs.

Information Processing. Mental activity of operating on information; an approach to studying cognition.

Information Transfer. Procedure by which information passes from transient to permanent store.

Insight Learning. Perception of relationships leading to solutions which can be applied in other settings, and which is unobservable.

Intelligence. Ability to acquire and use information in such a way as to demonstrate understanding of concrete and abstract ideas.

Interference. A theory of forgetting in which information competes for space.

Internal Lexicon. The mental dictionary.

Introspection. Consideration of the contents of one's mind, and the reports of that consideration.

IQ. A measure of ability on tests which is calculated as the ratio of a measured mental age to the chronological or actual age, multiplied by 100.

Knowledge Engineering. A specialised set of research methods designed to elicit knowledge from experts.

Knowledge Representation. Study of how information is stored and used.

Language Acquisition. The way in which we learn to use language. There are three major theories: the behaviourist, the innate and the information processing views.

Language Acquisition Device. Pre-programmed 'wiring' in the brain required for learning to use language in response to environmental stimuli.

Language Development. The way in which the use of language can be observed to change and the underlying skill development this implies.

Late Selection Model. Theory of attention in which selection of material is made in short term rather than sensory memory.

Latent Learning. Learning that takes place without being immediately manifest in behaviour.

Levels of Processing. A theory of how type and depth of processing affects retention.

Long Term or Permanent Store. A type of memory structure holding relatively large amounts of information, relatively permanently.

Machine Learning. Acquisition of new knowledge in order to improve performance.

Memory Codes. Evidence suggests that information is coded for organisation in transient store, codes being investigated including auditory, visual and semantic.

Mental Chronometry. Measurement of the time taken to perform mental processes.

Mental Model. Mental representation of the world and its state.

Monotonic Reasoning. Reasoning based on the assumption that once a fact is verified it cannot be altered during the reasoning process.

Morpheme. Smallest meaning unit of language.

Multistore Model. A theory of how several components of memory are linked and work together.

Noetic Consciousness. Knowing.

Non-monotonic Reasoning. Reasoning using multiple lines of thought allowing new facts or changed facts to be incorporated on the basis of new information.

Operant Conditioning. Learning in which positive reinforcement of a behaviour increases the probability of that behaviour being produced, or negative reinforcement decreases the probability.

Organic State. Brain dysfunction associated with amnesia, including head injury, strokes, alcoholism and degenerative diseases of the brain.

Parsing. Syntactic analysis of sentences, clauses or phrases.

Particular Affirmative. A feature of sets in which portions of categories are included.

Pattern Recognition. Identification of recurring combinations of environmental inputs.

Phone. Spoken phoneme.

Phoneme. Smallest sound unit of language.

Physical Symbol System. A system capable of storing and interpreting symbols.

Pragmatics. The intention of language.

Preconscious and Unconscious Memory. Different states of information, readily accessible, and unavailable respectively.

Predicate Calculus. A formalised logical language.

Primal Sketch. A cartoon-like description derived from the grey-level description.

Proactive Inhibition. Old material interfering with new.

Problem Solving. A process directed towards finding a solution when no method is readily available.

Procedural Knowledge. Knowledge about how to do things.

Production System. Mental system in which the knowledge is stored as production rules.

Productive Knowledge. Knowledge based on production systems.

Proposition. Smallest component of knowledge which can stand alone.

Propositional Model. Model in which knowledge is stored as propositions.

Prototype. Typical instance of a concept, the 'average'.

Psychogenic State. Psychiatric problem associated with amnesia.

Psychometrics. Study and use of standardised tests of ability and personality.

Psychophysics. Measurement and development of general laws to describe relationships between psychological experience and changes in continuums of stimuli.

Rationalism. Acquisition of knowledge through reasoning.

Recall. A retrieval process of reconstruction.

Recognition. A retrieval process of comparison.

Reinforcer. An environmental consequence of behaviour.

Release from Proactive Inhibition. A phenomenon in which it is more difficult to recall later items when earlier items have already been learnt.

Repression. Motivated forgetting due to memory being too painful for recall.

Reticular Activating Formation. A brain structure associated with awareness.

Retroactive Inhibition. New material interfering with old.

Retrograde Amnesia. Inability to recall past events.

Schemata, Frames and Scripts. Forms of organisation in permanent store.

Semantic Feature Comparison Model. Knowledge representation in which words become sets of features and members are compared.

Semantic Network Model. Hierarchical model of knowledge representation comprising nodes and attributes.

Semantic Priming. Phenomenon in which presentation of one word will bring about recall of related words.

Semantics. The meaning of words.

Sensory Store. A type of memory structure that holds information from the immediate environment.

Serial Position Effect. The effect seen when subjects recall word lists, with the first in the list (primacy effect) and the last in the list (recency effect) recalled better than the others.

Set-theoretical Model. A type of clustering model in which categories and attributes are stored together.

Shape from Shading. Apparent structure derived from drawn shading.

Short Term or Transient Store. A type of memory structure holding information from the present, limited in capacity and fragile in nature.

Skill. An ability to use specialised behaviour – motor, social or cognitive – to complete tasks.

Spreading Activation. The presentation of one item held in a semantic net will trigger the activation of the net close by.

State-Dependent Forgetting. Loss of information due to the retrieval state being different from the cueing state.

Stereopsis. Visual images from two eyes.

Sternberg Paradigm. An experimental procedure in which participants compare a probe with a memory set.

Strong AI. View that computers may have mental states and hence be intelligent.

Structure from Motion. Images are easier to see in motion.

Surface Structure. Order of words in sentences.

Syllogism. Set of logical statements.

Syntax. Structure of language.

Threshold. Point at which stimuli can be detected (absolute) or the difference between two stimuli can be detected (differential).

Trace-Dependent Forgetting. Loss of memory trace leads to forgetting.

Transduction. Process of converting energy at the sensory receptive field into neural impulses.

Transformational Grammar. Rules by which sentences are transformed into meaning, and meaning into sentences.

Turing Machine. An abstract machine which can read and write symbols, and change its internal state as a result.

Turing Test. A competitive method devised for identifying true AI.

Universal Affirmative. A feature of sets in which all members of a category are included.

Universal Turing Machine. A Turing Machine which can carry out the processes of any other given the same instructions.

Visual Acuity. Extent of the ability to see fine detail.

Visual Cortex. Area of the brain sensitive to visual input; there are also areas known to be receptive to auditory, olfactory, gustatory, somatosensory and proprioceptive input.

Visuo-spatial Sketch Pad A component of working memory concerned with visual and spatial information.

Weak AI. View that computers are only symbol manipulators, and whilst a useful tool for studying the mind, cannot be intelligent.

Wernicke's Encephalopathy. Degeneration in the brain leading to memory disorders. Associated with thiamine deficiency, often linked to alcoholism, when it is known as Korsakoff's syndrome, although this can have other causes than alcohol abuse.

Working Memory. A theory of how transient memory works.

Bibliography

Adams R., Maurer D. & Davis M. (1986) New-borns' discriminatin of chromatic from achromatic stimuli. *Journal of Experimental Child Psychology* **41** 267–81.

Aitchison J. (1983) *The Articulate Mammal: an Introduction to Psycholinguistics.* Universe: New York.

Alexander J. & Schwanenflugel P. (1994) Strategy regulation: the role of intelligence, metacognitive attribution and knowledge base. *Developmental Psychology* **30** 709–23.

Allport D. (1983) Language and cognition. In D. Harris (ed.) *Approaches to Language.* Pergamon: Oxford.

Anastasi A. & Urbina S. (1997) *Psychological Testing* (7th edn). Prentice Hall: Englewood Cliffs, New Jersey.

Anderson D., Choi H. & Lorch E. (1987) Attentional inertia reduces distractibility during young children's TV viewing. *Child Development* **58** 798–806.

Anderson J. (1976) *Language Memory and Thought.* Erlbaum: New Jersey.

Anderson J. (1983) Acquisition of proof skills in geometry. In J. Carbonel, R. Michalksi & T. Mitchell (eds) *Machine Learning: an Artificial Intelligence Approach.* Tioga Publishing: California.

Anderson J. (1996) A simple theory of complex cognition. *American Psychologist* **51**(4) 355–65.

Anderson J. & Bower G. (1973) *Human Associative Memory.* Winston: Washington DC.

Atkinson R. & Juola J. (1974) Search and decision processes in recognition memory. In D. Krantz, R. Atkinson & P. Suppes (eds) *Contemporary Developments in Mathematical Psychology.* Freeman: London.

Atkinson R. & Shiffrin R. (1968) Human memory: a proposed system and its control processes. In K. Spence & J. Spence (eds) *The Psychology of Learning and Motivation,* vol. 2. Academic Press: London.

Baddeley A. (1992) Working memory. *Science* **255**(5044) 556–9.

Baddeley A. & Hitch G. (1974) Working memory. In G. Bower (ed.) *The Psychology of Learning and Motivation,* vol. 8. Academic Press: London.

Bahrick H. (1970) Two-phase model for prompted recall. *Psychological Review* **77** 215–22.

Baillargeon R. & DeVos J. (1991) Object permanence in young infants: further evidence. *Child Development* **62** 122–46.

Bandura A. (1967) The role of modelling in personality development. In C. Lavatelli & F. Stendler (eds) *Readings in Childhood and Development.* Harcourt Brace Jovanovich: New York.

Bartlett F. (1932) *Remembering: a Study in Experimental and Social Psychology.* Cambridge University Press: Cambridge.

Jartlett F. (1958) *Thinking.* Basic Books: New York.

Bates E., Bretherton I. & Snyder L. (1988) *From First Words to Grammar: Individual Difference and Dissociable Mechanisms.* Cambridge University Press: Cambridge.

Beaumont J., Kenealy P. & Rogers M. (1996) *The Blackwell Dictionary of Neuropsychology.* Blackwell: Oxford.

Beletsky L., Higgins B. & Orians G. (1986) Communication by changing signals: call switching in red-winged blackbirds. *Behavioural Ecology and Sociobiology* **18** 221–9.

Bellazza F. (1993) Does 'perplexing' describe the self-reference effect? In Snill & Wyer (eds) *The Mental Representation of Trait and Autobiographical Knowledge about the Self: Advances in Social Cognition,* vol. 5. Lawrence Erlbaum: New Jersey.

Bench-Capon T. (1995) *Knowledge Representation: an Approach to Artificial Intelligence.* Academic Press: London.

Binet A. & Simon Th. (1905) Méthodes nouvelles pour le diagnostic du niveau intellectuel des anormaux. *Année Psychologique* **11** 191–244.

Bloom L. (1970) *Language Development: Form and Function in Merging Grammars.* MIT Press: Cambridge, Massachusetts.

Bobrow D. (1968) A Turing Test Passed. *ACM SIGART* Newsletter **Dec.** 14–15.

Bower G. (1970) Organisational factors in memory. *Cognitive Psychology* **1** 18–46.

Brachman R. (1979) On the epistemological status of semantic networks. In N. Findler (ed.) *Associative Networks: Representation and Use of Knowledge by Computers.* Academic Press: New York.

Bradley D. & Petry H. (1977) Organisational determinants of subjective contour: the subjective Necker cube. *American Journal of Psychology* **90** 253–62.

Bransford J., McCarell N., Franks J. & Nitsch K. (1977) Towards explaining memory. In R. Shaw & J. Bransford (eds) *Perceiving, Acting and Knowing.* Lawrence Erlbaum: New Jersey.

Broadbent D. (1958) *Perception and Communication.* Pergamon Press: London.

Broadbent D. (1984) The Maltese Cross: a new simplistic model for memory. *Behavioural and Brain Sciences* **7** 55–94.

Brown G. & Yule G. (1983) *Discourse Analysis.* Cambridge University Press: Cambridge.

Brown R. & McNeill D. (1966) The 'tip of the tongue' phenomenon. *Journal of Verbal Learning and Verbal Behaviour* **5** 325–37.

Bruner J., Goodnow J. & Austin G. (1956) *A Study of Thinking.* Wiley: New York.

Burgess C. & Chiarello C. (1996) Neurocognitive mechanisms underlying metaphor comprehension and other figurative language. *Metaphor and Symbolic Activity* **11**(6) 67–84.

Butterworth B. (1975) Hesitation and semantic planning in speech. *Journal of Psycholinguistic Research* **4** 75–87.

Campbell F. & Robson J. (1968) Application of Fourier analysis to the visibility of gratings. *Journal of Physiology* **197** 551–66.

Carlson N. (1991) *Physiology of Behaviour.* Allyn & Bacon: New York.

Chase W. & Ericsson K. (1982) Skill and working memory. In G. Bower (ed.) *The Psychology of Learning and Motivation,* vol. 6. Academic Press: London.

Chase W. & Simon H. (1973) Perceptions in chess. *Cognitive Psychology* **4** 58–81.

Cherry E. (1953) Some experiments on the recognition of speech with one and two ears. *Journal of the Acoustical Society of America* **25** 975–9.

Chomsky N. (1957) *Syntactic Structures*. Moutin: The Hague.

Chomsky N. (1959) Review of Skinner's verbal behaviour. *Language* **35** 26–58.

Chomsky N. (1972) *Language and Mind*. Harcourt Brace Jovanovich: New York.

Chomsky N. (1986) *Knowledge of Language: Its Nature, Origins and Use*. Praeger: New York.

Cole M. & Scribner S. (1977) Cross-cultural studies of memory and cognition. In R. Vail Jr. & J. Hagen (eds) *Perspectives on the Development of Memory and Recognition*. Erlbaum: New Jersey.

Collins A. & Loftus E. (1975) A spreading activation theory of semantic processing. *Psychological Review* **82** 407–28.

Collins A. & Quillian M. (1969) Retrieval time from semantic memory. *Journal of Verbal Learning and Verbal Behaviour* **11** 671–84.

Coltheart M., Patterson K. & Marshall J. (1987) *Deep Dyslexia*. Routledge: London.

Compton B. & Logan G. (1991) The transition from algorithm to retrieval in memory based theories of automaticity. *Memory and Cognition* **19**(2) 151–8.

Conrad C. (1972) Cognitive economy in semantic memory. *Journal of Experimental Psychology*, **92** 149–54.

Conrad R. (1963) Acoustic confusions and memory span for words. *Nature* **197** 1029–30.

Costermans J., Lories G. & Ansay C. (1992) Confidence level and feeling of knowing in question answering: the weight of inferential processes. *Journal of Experimental Psychology: Learning, Memory and Cognition* **18** 142–50.

Craik F. & Lockhart R. (1972) Levels of processing: a framework for memory research. *Journal of Verbal Learning and Verbal Behaviour* **11** 671–84.

Critchley M. (1970) *The Dyslexic Child*. Heinemann: London.

Cullinan V., Barnes D., Hampson P. & Lyddy F. (1994) A transfer of explicitly and non-explicitly trained sequence responses through equivalence relations: experimental demonstration and a connectionist model. *Psychological Record* **44** 559–85.

Darwin C. (1872) *The Expression of Emotions in Man and Animals*. John Murray: London.

D'Esposito M., Detre J., Alsop D. & Shin R. (1995) The neural basis of the central executive system of working memory. *Nature* **378**(6554) 279–81.

Deutsch C. & Kinsbourne M. (1990) Genetics and biochemistry in attention deficit disorder. In M. Lewis & S. Miller (eds) *Handbook of Developmental Psychopathology*. Plenum: New York.

Deutsch F. & Deutsch D. (1963) Attention: some theoretical considerations. *Psychological Review* **70** 80–90.

Donders F. (1868) Work in the Physiological Laboratory of Utrecht Hoogeschool.

Duncker K. (1945) On problem solving. *Psychological Monographs* **58**(5) (whole number 270).

Ebbinghaus H. (1885) *Über das Gedachtnis*. Duncker: Leipzig.

Eich E. & Metcalfe J. (1989) Mood dependent memory for internal versus external events. *Journal of Experimental Psychology: Learning, Memory and Cognition* **15** 443–55.

Ellis A. & Beattie G. (1986) *The Psychology of Language and Communication.* Weidenfeld & Nicolson: London.

Evans T. (1968) A program for the solution of geometric-analogy intelligence test questions. In M. Minsky (ed.) *Semantic Information Processing.* MIT Press: Cambridge, Massachusetts.

Fahlman S. (1979) *NETL: a System for Representing and Using Real-World Knowledge.* MIT Press: Cambridge, Massachusetts.

Fechner G. (1876) *Vorschule der Aesthetik.* Breitkopf und Hartel: Leipzig.

Feigenbaum J., Polkey C. & Morris R. (1996) Deficits in spatial working memory after unilateral temporal lobectomy in man. *Neuropsychologia* **34**(3) 163–76.

Field D. (1987) Relations between the statistics of natural images and the response properties of cortical cells. *Journal of the Optical Society of America* **A4** 2379–94.

Fisher R. & Geiselman R.(1988) Enhancing eyewitness testimony with the cognitive interview. In M. Gruenberg, P. Morris & R. Sykes (eds) *Practical Aspects of Memory: Current Research and Issues.* Wiley: Chichester.

Fitts P. & Posner M. (1967) *Human Performance.* Brooks-Cole: California.

Fodor J. & Pylyshyn Z. (1988) Connectionism and cognitive architecture. *Cognition* **28** 3–71.

Foss D. (1982) A discourse on semantic priming. *Cognitive Psychology* **14** 590–607.

Frege G. (1879/1972) Conceptual notation: a formula language of pure thought modelled upon the formula language of arithmetic. In T. Bynum (ed. and trans.) *Conceptual Notation and Related Articles.* Oxford University Press: Oxford. Paper first published in German in 1879 by L. Nerbet, Halle.

Friederici A. (1995) The time course of syntactic activation during language processing: a model based on neuropsychological and neurophysiological data. *Brain and Language* **50**(3) 259–81.

Galaburda A. (1989) *From Reading to Neurones: Toward Theory and Methods for Research on Developmental Dyslexia.* MIT Press: Cambridge, Massachusetts.

Galton F. (1869) *Hereditary Genius: an Inquiry into its Laws and Consequences.* Macmillan: New York.

Gandevia S., McCloskey D. & Burke D. (1992) Kinaesthetic signals and muscle contraction. *Trends in Neuroscience* **115** 62–5.

Gardner H. (1983) *Frames of Mind: the Theory of Multiple Intelligences.* Basic Books: New York.

Gavin H. (1992) *Selection Interviewing: a Study in Applied Knowledge Engineering.* Unpublished doctoral thesis, University of Teesside.

Gibson J. (1979) *The Ecological Approach to Visual Perception.* Houghton Mifflin: Boston, Massachusetts.

Glanzer M. & Cunitz A. (1966) Two storage mechanisms in free recall. *Journal of Verbal Learning and Verbal Behaviour* **11** 403–16.

Godden D. & Baddeley A. (1975) Context-dependent memory in two natural environments. *British Journal of Psychology* **66** 325–31.

Goldman-Eisler F. (1968) The predictability of words in context and the length of pauses in speech. *Journal of Communication* **11** 95–9.

Goldman-Rakic P. (1987) Development of cortical circuitry and cognitive function. *Child Development* **58** 601–22.

Graf P., Squire L. & Mandler G. (1984) The information that amnesiac patients do not forget. *Journal of Experimental Psychology: Learning, Memory and Cognition* **10** 164–78.

Gregory R. (1972) Seeing as thinking. *Times Literary Supplement* 23 June.

Grice H. (1975) Logic and conversation. In P. Cole & J. Morgan (eds) *Syntax and Semantics 3: Speech Acts.* Academic Press: New York.

Guillem F., N'Kaoua B., Rougier, A. & Claverie B. (1996) Differential involvement of the human temporal lobe structures in short- and long-term memory processes assessed by intracranial ERPs. *Psychophysiology* 33(6) 720–30.

Halpern A. & Bower G. (1982) Musical expertise and melodic structure in memory for musical notation. *American Journal of Psychology* 95 31–50.

Hamann S. & Squire L. (1996) Level-of-processing effects in word-completion priming: a neuropsychological study. *Journal of Experimental Psychology: Learning, Memory and Cognition* 22(4) 933–47.

Harder D., Maggio J. & Whitney G. (1989) Assessing gustatory detection capabilities using preference procedures. *Chemical Senses* 14 547–64.

Harris M. & Coltheart M. (1986) *Language Processing in Children and Adults: an Introduction to Psycholinguistics.* Routledge & Kegan Paul: London.

Hayes J. (1978) *Cognitive Psychology: Thinking and Creating.* Dorsey Press: Illinois.

Hayes-Roth F. (1985) Knowledge-based expert systems – the state of the art in the US. *Knowledge Engineering Review* 1(2) 18–27.

Hebb D. (1949) *The Organization of Behaviour.* Wiley: New York.

Helmholtz H. von (1909) Treatise on physiological optics. Published in 1962. English translation by Dover, New York.

Hillis W. (1985) *The Connection Machine.* MIT Press: Cambridge, Massachusetts.

Hinton G, Plaut D. & Shallice T. (1993) Simulating brain damage. *Scientific American* 269(3) 145–51.

Holmes J., Mattingly I. & Shearme J. (1964) Speech synthesis by rule. *Language and Speech* 7 127–43.

Howard D. & Hatfield F. (1987) *Aphasia Therapy: Historical and Contemporary Issues.* Lawrence Erlbaum: London.

Hubel D. & Wiesel T. (1962) Receptive fields, binocular interaction and functional architecture in the cat's visual cortex. *Journal of Physiology* 160 106–54.

Hubel D. & Wiesel T. (1979) Brain mechanism of vision. *Scientific American* 241 150–62.

Hunt E. (1978) Mechanics of verbal ability. *Psychological Review* 85 109–30.

Huss M. & Weaver K. (1996) Effect of modality in earwitness identification: memory for verbal and non-verbal auditory stimuli presented in two contexts. *Journal of General Psychology* 123(4) 277–87.

Isard S. & Miller D. (1986) Diphone synthesis techniques. *Proceedings of the IEEE International Conference of Speech Input/Output Techniques and Applications,* 77–82.

James W. (1890) *The Principles of Psychology.* Holt: New York.

Jamison K. (1994) *Touched with Fire.* Free Press: New York.

Jenkins J. & Dallenbach K. (1924) Obliviscence during sleep and waking. *American Journal of Psychology* 35 605–12.

Johnson L. & Johnson N. (1988) Teachback interviews: knowledge elicitation in VLSI. In A. Kidd (ed.) *Knowledge Acquisition for Expert Systems.* Plenum Press: New York.

Johnson-Laird P. (1983) *Mental Models: Towards a Cognitive Science of Language, Inference and Consciousness.* Cambridge University Press: Cambridge.

Johnson-Laird P. (1988) Mental models. In M. Posner (ed.) *Foundations of Cognitive Science.* MIT Press: Cambridge, Massachusetts.

Johnston W., Dark V. & Jacoby L. (1985) Perceptual fluency and recognition judgements. *Journal of Experimental Psychology: Learning, Memory and Cognition* **11** 3–11.

Johnston W. & Heinz S. (1978) Flexibility and capacity demands of attention. *Journal of Experimental Psychology: General* **107** 420–35.

Jones G. (1987) Independence and exclusivity among psychological processes: implications for the structure of recall. *Psychological Review* **94** 229–35.

Kahneman D. (1973) *Attention and Effort.* Prentice Hall: New Jersey.

Kahneman D. & Tversky A. (1982) Papers in D. Kahneman, P. Slovic & A. Tversky (eds) *Judgement under Uncertainty: Heuristics and Biases.* Cambridge University Press: Cambridge.

Kelly G. (1955) *The Psychology of Personal Constructs.* Norton: New York.

Köhler W. (1925) *The Mentality of Apes.* Harcourt Brace: New York.

Kopelmann M. (1995) The Korsakoff syndrome. *British Journal of Psychiatry* **166** 154–77.

Kopelmann M., Wilson B. and Baddeley A. (1990) *The Autobiographical Memory Interview.* Thames Valley Test Company: Bury St Edmunds.

Krumhansl C. (1990) *Cognitive Foundations of Musical Pitch.* Oxford University Press: New York.

Larkin J. (1981) Enriching formal knowledge: a model for learning to solve textbook problems. In J. Anderson (ed.) *Cognitive Skills and their Acquisition.* Erlbaum: New Jersey.

Larkin J., McDermott, J., Simon D. & Simon H. (1988) Expert and novice performance in solving physics problems. *Science* **208** 1335–42.

Lashley K. (1929) *Brain Mechanisms and Intelligence.* University of Chicago Press: Chicago.

Lei X. (1991) The parallel processing in understanding natural language. *Acta Psychologica Sinica* **23**(2) 158–66.

Lenat D. (1983) AM: discovery in mathematics as heuristic search. In R. Davis & D. Lenat (eds) *Knowledge-based Systems in Artificial Intelligence.* McGraw Hill: New York.

Lenneberg E. (1967) *Biological Foundation of Language.* Wiley: New York.

Lewis J. (1970) Semantic processing of unattended messages using dichotic listening. *Journal of Experimental Psychology* **85** 225–8.

Lim S. & Lippman L. (1991) Mental practice and memorisation of piano music. *Journal of General Psychology* **118**(1) 21–30.

Lindberg M. (1980) Is knowledge base development a necessary and sufficient condition for memory development? *Journal of Experimental Child Psychology* **30** 401–10.

Lindsay D. & Johnson M. (1989) The eyewitness suggestibility effect and memory for source. *Memory and Cognition* **17** 349–58.

Livingstone M. & Hubel D. (1988) Segregation of form, colour, movement and depth: anatomy, physiology and perception. *Science* **240** 740–9.

Loftus E. (1975) Leading questions and the eyewitness report. *Cognitive Psychology* **7** 560–72.

Loftus E. (1979) *Eyewitness Testimony.* Harvard University Press: Massachusetts.

Luria A. (1968) *The Mind of a Mnemonist.* Basic Books: New York.

Macfarlane A. (1975) Olfaction in the development of social preference in the human neonate. In *Parent–Infant Interaction* (CIBA Foundation Symposium 33). Elsevier: Amsterdam.

Mackintosh N. (1983) *Conditioning and Associative Learning.* Oxford University Press: Oxford.

Mandler G. (1967) Organisation and memory. In K. Spence & J. Spence (eds) *The Psychology of Learning and Motivation: Advances in Research and Theory*, vol. 1. Academic Press: London.

Mann T. & Brenner L. (1996) Improving text memory by organizing interfering text at retrieval. *American Journal of Psychology* **109**(4) 539–49.

Marcus M. (1980) *A Theory of Syntactic Recognition for Natural Language.* MIT Press: Cambridge, Massachusetts.

Margolskee R. (1995) Receptor mechanisms in gustation. In R. Dory (ed.) *Handbook of Olfaction and Gustation.* Marcel Dekker: New York.

Marr D. (1982) *Vision: a Computational Investigation into the Human Representation and Processing of Visual Information.* Freeman: San Francisco.

McClelland J. (1981) Retrieving general and specific knowledge from stored knowledge of specifics. *Proceedings of the 3rd Annual Conference of the Cognitive Science Society*, 170–2.

McClelland J. & Rumelhart D. (1981) An interactive activation model of context effects in letter perception: Part I. An account of basic findings. *Psychological Review* **88** 375–407.

McClelland J. & Rumelhart D. (1988) *Exploration in Parallel Distributed Processing: a Handbook of Models, Programs and Exercises.* MIT Press: Cambridge, Massachusetts.

McNally R., Lasko N., Macklin M. & Pitman R. (1995) Autobiographical memory disturbance in combat related post-traumatic stress disorder. *Behaviour Research and Therapy* **33**(6) 19–30.

Mecklinger A. & Muller N. (1996) Dissociations in the processing of 'what' and 'where' information in working memory: an event-related potential analysis. *Journal of Cognitive Neuroscience* **8**(5) 453–73.

Medin D. (1989) Concepts and conceptual structures. *American Psychologist* **44** 1469–81.

Medin D. & Shoben E. (1988) Context and structure in conceptual combination. *Cognitive Psychology* **20** 158–90.

Meyer R. (1983) *Thinking, Problem-solving, Cognition.* Freeman: New York.

Michalski R. (1983) A Theory and Methodology of Inductive Learning. *Artificial Intelligence* **20**.

Miles T. (1989) The work of the dyslexia group at Bangor. *The Psychologist.*

Miller G. (1956) The magical number seven plus or minus two: some limits on our capacity for processing information. *Psychological Review* **63** 81–97.

Miller G. & Johnson-Laird P. (1976) *Language and Perception.* Cambridge University Press: Cambridge.

Miller G. & McKean J.(1964) A chronometric study of some relations between sentences. *Quarterly Journal of Experimental Psychology* **16** 297–308.

Miller N. (1985) The value of behavioural research on animals. *American Psychologist* **40** 423–40.

Mistlin A. & Perret D. (1990) Visual and somatosensory processing in the macaque temporal cortex: the role of 'expectation'. *Experimental Brain Research* **82** 437–50.

Mitchell T. (1982) Generalisation as search. *Artificial Intelligence* **18** 203–6.

Mitchell T., Utgoff P. & Banerji R. (1983) Learning by experimentation: acquiring and refining problem solving heuristics. In R. Michalksi, J. Carbonel & T. Mitchell (eds) *Machine Learning: an Artificial Intelligence Approach*. Tioga Publishing: California.

Moray N. (1959) Attention in dichotic listening: affective cues and the influence of instructions. *Quarterly Journal of Experimental Psychology* **11** 56–60.

Morgan J. (1990) Input, innateness and induction in language acquisition. *Developmental Psychobiology* **23** 661–79.

Mostow D. (1983) Machine transformation of advice into a heuristic search procedure. In R. Michalksi, J. Carbonel & T. Mitchell (eds) *Machine Learning: an Artificial Intelligence Approach*. Tioga Publishing: California.

Mountcastle V. (1978) Brain mechanisms of directed attention. *Journal of the Royal Society of Medicine* **71** 4–27.

Mowrer O. & Mowrer W. (1938) Enuresis: a method for its study and treatment. *American Journal of Orthopsychiatry* **8** 436–7.

Mumford M. & Gustafson S. (1988) Creativity syndrome: integration, application and innovation. *Psychological Bulletin* **103** 27–43.

Neisser U. (1967) *Cognitive Psychology*. Appleton-Century-Crofts: New York.

Neisser U. (1976) *Cognition and Reality*. Freeman: San Francisco.

Newell A. & Simon H. (1963) GPS, a program that simulates human thought. In E. Fiegenbaum & J. Feldman (eds) *Computers and Thought*. McGraw-Hill: New York.

Newell A. & Simon H. (1976) Computer science as empirical inquiry: symbols and search. In J. Haugeland (ed., 1981) *Mind Design: Philosophy, Psychology, Artificial Intelligence*. MIT Press: Cambridge, Massachusetts.

Norman D. (1980) Copycat science or does the mind really work by table look-up. In R. Cole (ed.) *Perception and Production of Fluent Speech*. Lawrence Erlbaum: New Jersey.

Norman D. & Shallice T. (1980) Attention to action: willed and automatic control of behaviour. *University of California, San Diego CHIP report 99*.

Ornstein R. (1977) *The Psychology of Consciousness*. Harcourt Brace Jovanovich: New York.

Overton D. (1984) State dependent learning and drug discriminations. In L. Iverson, S. Iverson & S. Snyder (eds) *Handbook of Psychopharmacology*, vol. 18. Plenum: New York.

Owings D. & Hennessy D. (1984) The importance of variation in sciurid visual and vocal communication. In J. Murie & G. Michener (eds) *The Biology of Ground Dwelling Squirrels*. University of Nebraska Press: Lincoln, NB.

Paivio A. (1971) *Imagery and Verbal Processes*. Holt, Rinehart & Winston: New York.

Paivio A. (1979) Psychological processes in the comprehension of metaphor. In A. Ortony (ed.) *Metaphor and Thought*. Cambridge University Press: Cambridge.

Pask G. (1975) *Conversation Cognition and Learning: a Cybernetic Theory and Methodology*. Elsevier: Amsterdam.

Patel V. & Groen G. (1986) Knowledge based solution strategies in medical reasoning. *Cognitive Science* **10** 91–116.

Pavlov I. (1927) *Conditioned Reflexes*. Oxford University Press: Oxford.

Payne J. (1976) Task complexity and contingent processing in decision making: an information search and protocol analysis. *Organisational Behaviour and Human Performance* **16** 366–87.

Penfield W. (1959) The interpretive cortex. *Science* 129 1719–25.

Penfield W. & Milner B. (1958) Memory deficit produced by bilateral lesions in the hippocampal zone. *Archives of Neurology and Psychiatry* 79 475–97.

Peterson C. & Seligman M. (1984) Causal explanation as a risk factor for depression: theory and evidence. *Psychological Review* 91 347–74.

Peterson L. & Peterson M. (1959) Short-term retention of individual verbal items. *Journal of Experimental Psychology* 58 193–8.

Piaget J. (1954) *The Construction of Reality in the Child* (trans. M. Cook), Basic Books: New York.

Piaget J. (1959) *Language and Thought of the Child.* Routledge & Kegan Paul: London.

Pinker S. (1994) *The Language Instinct: How the Mind Creates Language.* Harper Collins: New York.

Pinker S. & Prince A. (1988) On language and connectionism: analysis of a parallel distributed processing model of language acquisition. In S. Pinker & J. Mehler (eds) *Connections and Symbols.* MIT Press: Cambridge, Massachusetts.

Polanyi M. (1958) *Personal Knowledge.* University of Chicago Press: Chicago.

Pomerantz J. (1985) Perceptual organisation in information processing. In A. Aitkenhead & J. Slack (eds) *Issues in Cognitive Modelling.* Lawrence Erlbaum: London.

Popper K. (1959) *The Logic of Scientific Discovery.* Hutchinson: London.

Posner M. (1969) Abstraction and the process of recognition. In G. Bower & J. Spence (eds) *The Psychology of Learning and Motivation,* vol. 3. Academic Press: New York.

Posner M. (1988) Structures and function of selective attention. In T. Boll & B. Bryant (eds) *Master Lectures in Clinical Neuropsychology.* American Psychological Society, Washington DC.

Posner M. & Boies S. (1971) Abstraction and the process of recognition. In G. Bower & J. Spence (eds) *The Psychology of Learning and Motivation,* vol. 3. Academic Press: New York.

Posner M. & Petersen S. (1990) The attention system of the human brain. *Annual Review of Neuroscience* 13 25–42.

Posner M., Boies S, Eichelman W. & Taylor R. (1969) Retention of visual and name codes of single letter. *Journal of Experimental Psychology Monograph* 79 1–16.

Premack A. & Premack D. (1972) Teaching language to an ape. *Scientific American* 227 92–9.

Premack A. & Premack D. (1983) *The Mind of an Ape.* Norton: New York.

Reder L. & Ross B. (1983) Integrated knowledge in different tasks: positive and negative fan effects. *Journal of Experimental Psychology: Human Learning and Memory* 8 55–72.

Rescorla R. (1992) Hierarchical associative relations in Pavlovian conditioning and instrumental training. *Current Directions in Psychological Science* 1 66–70.

Rosch E. (1975) Cognitive representation of semantic categories. *Journal of Experimental Psychology: General* 104 192–233.

Rosenbloom P., Liard J., Newell A. and McCarl R. (1991) A preliminary analysis of the foundations of Soar. *Artificial Intelligence* 47 289–325.

Rosenweig M. (1996) Aspects of the search for the neural mechanisms of memory. *Annual Review of Psychology* 47 1–32.

Rossi J. (1992) Cognitive sciences and the minds of animals. *International Journal of Comparative Psychology* **6**(2) 113–15.

Rotter J. (1954) *Social Learning and Clinical Psychology.* Prentice Hall: New Jersey.

Rotter J. (1990) Internal vs. external control of reinforcement: a case history of a variable. *American Psychologist* **45** 489–93.

Rumelhart D. & Norman D. (1978) Accretion, tuning and restructuring: three modes of learning. In J. Cotton & R. Klatsky (eds) *Semantic Factors in Cognition.* Lawrence Erlbaum: New Jersey

Rumelhart D. & Zipser D. (1985) Feature discovery by competitive learning. *Cognitive Science* **9** 115–35.

Rundus D. (1977) Maintenance rehearsal and single-level processing. *Journal of Verbal Learning and Verbal Behaviour* **16** 665–81.

Sadowski M. & Quast Z. (1990) Reader response and long-term recall for journalistic test: the roles of imagery, affect and importance. *Reading Research Quarterly* **25** 221–3.

Samuel A. (1963) Some studies in machine learning using the game of checkers. In E. Fiegenbaum & J. Feldman (eds) *Computers and Thought.* Appleton-Century-Crofts: New York.

Savage-Rumbaugh E. (1990) Language acquisition in a non-human species: implications for the innateness debate. *Developmental Psychology* **23** 599–620.

Schachter D. (1983) Amnesia observed: remembering and forgetting in a natural environment. *Journal of Abnormal Psychology* **92** 236–42.

Schachter D., Glisky E. & McGlynn S. (1990) Impact of memory disorder on everyday life: awareness of deficits and return to work. In D. Tupper & K. Cicerone (eds) *The Neuropsychology of Everyday Life: Assessment and Basic Competencies.* Kluwer Academic Publishing: Boston.

Schachter D., Wang P., Tulving E. & Freedman M. (1982) Functional retrograde amnesia: a quantitative case study. *Neuropsychologia* **20** 523–32.

Schaeffer B. & Wallace R. (1970) The comparison of word meanings. *Journal of Experimental Psychology* **86** 144–52.

Schank R. (1975) Conceptual dependency: a theory of natural language understanding. *Cognitive Psychology* **3** 552–631.

Schank R. & Abelson R. (1977) *Scripts, Plans, Goals, and Understanding.* Lawrence Erlbaum: New Jersey.

Schnieder W. & Shiffrin R. (1977) Controlled and automatic human information processing: I Detection, search and attention. *Psychological Review* **84** 1–66.

Searle J. (1980) Minds, brains and programs. *Behavioural and Brain Sciences* **3** 417–24.

Seidenberg M. & McClelland J. (1989) A distributed developmental model of visual word recognition and pronunciation: acquisition, skilled performance and dyslexia. In A. Galaburda (ed.) *From Reading to Neurones: Toward Theory and Methods for Research on Developmental Dyslexia.* MIT Press: Cambridge, Massachusetts.

Seidenberg M. & Petitto L. (1987) Communication, symbolic communication and language: comment on Savage-Rumbaugh, McDonald, Sevcik, Hopkins and Rupert (1986). *Journal of Experimental Psychology: General* **116** 279–357.

Sekular R. & Blake R. (1994) *Perception.* McGraw-Hill: Cambridge, New York.

Seligman M. (1975) *Helplessness: on Depression Development and Death.* Freeman: San Francisco.

Seltzer A. (1994) Multiple personality: a psychiatric misadventure. *Canadian Journal of Psychiatry* **39** 442–5.

Shallice T. (1972) On the dual functions of consciousness. *Psychological Review* **79** 383–96.

Shaw M. (1981) *Recent Advances in Personal Construct Technology.* Academic Press: New York.

Short D., Workman E., Morse J. & Turner R. (1992) Mnemonics for eight DSM-III-R disorders. *Hospital and Community Psychiatry* **43** 642–4.

Simmons J. (1981) Project sea hunt: a report on prototype development and test. *Technical report no. 746.* Naval Ocean System Center: California.

Simon H. (1957) *Models of Man: Social and National.* Wiley: London.

Skinner B. (1938) *The Behaviour of Organisms.* Appleton-Century-Crofts: New York.

Skinner B. (1957) *Verbal Behaviour.* Appleton-Century-Crofts: New York.

Slack J. (1984) Cognitive science research. In T. O'Shea & M. Einstadt (eds) *AI: Tools, Techniques and Applications.* Harper & Row: London.

Slater A. (1989) Visual perception and memory in early infancy. In A. Slater & G. Bremner (eds) *Infant Development.* Erlbaum: Sussex.

Slobin D. (1966) Grammatical transformation and sentence comprehension in children and adults. *Journal of Verbal Learning and Verbal Behaviour* **5** 291–301.

Sloboda J. (1991) Musical expertise. In K. Anders, K. Ericsson & J. Smith (eds) *Towards a General Theory of Expertise: Prospects and Limits.* Cambridge University Press: Cambridge.

Sloboda J., Davidson J. & Howe M. (1994a) Is everyone musical? Target paper, *The Psychologist* **7**(8) 349–54.

Sloboda J., Davidson J. & Howe M. (1994b) Musicians: experts not geniuses. Reply paper, *The Psychologist* **7**(8) 363–4.

Smith S., Shoben E. & Rips L. (1974) Structure and process in semantic memory: a feature model for semantic decision. *Psychological Review* **81** 214–41.

Sokolov E. (1960) Neuronal models and the orienting reflexes. In M. Brazier (ed.) *The Central Nervous System and Behaviour.* Macy: New York.

Spearman C. (1927) *The Abilities of Man.* Macmillan: New York.

Spelke E., Hirst W. & Neisser U. (1976). Skills of divided attention. *Cognition* **4** 215–30.

Sperber D. & Wilson D. (1986) *Relevance, Communication and Cognition.* Blackwell: Oxford.

Sperling G. (1960) The information available in brief visual presentations. *Psychological Monographs* **174** (whole number 498).

Squire L. (1986) Mechanisms of memory. *Science* **232** 1612–19.

Squire L., Zola-Morgan S., Cave C., Haist H., Musen G. & Suzuki W. (1990) Memory: organisation of brain systems and cognition. In E. Kandel, T. Sejnowski, C. Stevens & J. Watson (eds) *Cold Spring Harbor Symposia Quarterly Biol.* **55**.

Sternberg R. (1977) *Intelligence, Information Processing and Analogical Reasoning: the Componential Analysis of Human Abilities.* Erlbaum: New Jersey.

Sternberg R. & Frensch P. (1990) Intelligence and cognition. In M. Eysenck (ed.) *International Review of Cognitive Psychology.* Wiley: Chichester.

Sternberg S. (1966) High speed scanning in human memory. *Science* **153** 652–4.

Sternberg S. (1969) The discovery of processing stages: extensions to Donders' method. *Acta Psychologica* **30** 276–315.

Strachey J. (1957) *The Standard Edition of the Complete Psychological Works of Sigmund Freud*. Hogarth Press: London.

Stroop J. (1935) Studies of interference in serial verbal reactions. *Journal of Experimental Psychology* **18** 634–62.

Sussman G. (1975) *A Computer Model of Skill Acquisition*. American Elsevier: New York.

Swets J. (1992) The science of choosing the right decision threshold in high-stakes diagnostics. *American Psychologist* **47** 522–32.

Thomson M. (1984) *Developmental Dyslexia*. Blackwell: Oxford.

Thorndike E. (1898) Animal intelligence: an experimental study of the associative processes in animals. *Psychological Review Monograph supplement* **2**(8).

Thorndike E. (1911) *Animal Intelligence: Experimental Studies*. MacMillan: New York.

Thorne J., Bratley P. & Dewar H. (1968) The syntactic analysis of English by machine. In D. Michie (ed.) *Machine Intelligence 3*. Edinburgh University Press: Edinburgh.

Tolman E. (1948) Cognitive maps in rats and men. *Psychological Review* **55** 189–208.

Treisman A. (1960) Contextual cues in selective listening. *Quarterly Journal of Experimental Psychology* **12** 242–8.

Treisman A. (1969) Strategies and models of selective attention. *Psychological Review* **78** 282–99.

Tulving E. (1972) Episodic and semantic memory. In E. Tulving & W. Donaldson (eds) *Organisation of Memory*. Academic Press: New York.

Tulving E. (1974) Cue dependent forgetting. *American Scientist* **62** 74–82.

Tulving E. (1985) Memory and consciousness. *Canadian Psychologist* **26** 1–11.

Tulving E. (1989) Remembering and knowing the past. *American Scientist* **77** 361–7.

Tulving E. & Schachter D. (1990) Priming and human memory systems. *Science* **247** 301–6.

Tulving E. and Thomson D. (1973) Encoding specificity and retrieval processes in episodic memory. *Psychological Review* **80** 79–82.

Turing A. (1936) On computable numbers, with an application to the Entscheidungsproblem. *Proceedings of the London Mathematical Society* **Series 2, 42** (1936–7) 230–65.

Turing A. (1950) Computing machinery and intelligence. *Mind* **59** 433–50.

Tversky A. (1972) Elimination by aspects. *Psychological Review* **79** 281–99.

Ullman S. (1979) *The Interpretation of Visual Motion*. MIT Press: Cambridge, Massachusetts.

Wakefield J. (1991) The outlook for creativity tests. *Journal of Creative Behaviour* **25** 184–93.

Wason P. (1965) The contexts of plausible denial. *Journal of Verbal Learning and Verbal Behaviour* **4** 7–11.

Watson J. (1930) *Behaviourism* (rev. edn). Norton: New York.

Wechsler D. (1987) *Wechsler Memory Scale Revised*. Psychological Corporation: New York.

Weilinga B. & Breuker J. (1986) Models of expertise. *Proc. EXAI '86* **1** 306–18.

Weist R. (1972) The role of rehearsal: recopy or reconstruct. *Journal of Verbal Learning and Verbal Behaviour* **11** 440–50.

Weizenbaum J. (1966) ELIZA – a computer program for the study of natural language communication between man and machine. *Communications of the Association for Computing Machinery* **9** 336–45.

Wertheimer M. (1959) *Productive Thinking*. Harper & Row: New York.

White D. (1992) The cat (*Felis catus*) as an example of the contribution that comparative psychology has made to human factors. *International Journal of Comparative Psychology* 5(4) 167–78.

Whitten W. & Leonard J. (1981) Directed search through autobiographical memory. *Memory and Cognition* 9 566–79.

Wickens D., Born D. & Allen C. (1963) Proactive inhibition and item similarity in short term memory. *Journal of Verbal Learning and Verbal Behaviour* 2 440–5.

Wilson B. (1987) *Rehabilitation of Memory*. Guilford Press: New York.

Woods W. (1977) Transition network grammars for natural language analysis. *Communications of the Association for Computing Machinery* 13 591–606.

Wundt W. (1912) *An Introduction to Psychology*. Allen: London.

Index